EXPLORING MATHEMATICS
— with —
SPREADSHEETS

Lulu Healy and Rosamund Sutherland

Blackwell Education

First published 1991
Published by
Basil Blackwell Limited
108 Cowley Road
Oxford OX4 1JF

Reprinted 1991

British Library Cataloguing in Publication Data
Healy, Lulu
  Exploring mathematics with spreadsheets.
  1. Mathematics. Applications of microcomputer systems.
  Spreadsheet packages
  I. Title II. Sutherland, Rosamund
  510.285536

  ISBN 0-631-90544-8

Printed in Great Britain by Martin's of Berwick

Contents

List of activities

Acknowledgements

Firstly we would like to thank all the pupils and teachers who tried out the materials presented in this book. Without them we would not have been able to develop our ideas and gain insight into the potential of a spreadsheet for learning mathematics. We are particularly grateful to the following teachers who supported us in our work in the classroom: Ann Edwards and Tony Edey of Fortismere School, Haringey; Jane Harris of Townsend C. of E. School, St. Albans and Liz Hemming of The Priory School, Hitchin. A number of teachers who have attended in-service courses at the Institute of Education have also played an important role in the development of our ideas and these include John Eyles, Richard Hale, Adelaide Lister, Lema Mani, Veronica Peters and Andrew Seager.

We are also grateful to Bernard Capponi from the University of Grenoble who provided us with some very important ideas when we first started our spreadsheet work.

We would like to thank all our colleagues at the Institute of Education who have always been receptive to our 'half-formed' ideas. In particular Celia Hoyles who worked with us on the 'Peer Group Discussion in Mathematical Environments' Project which was the starting point for our spreadsheet work. More recently Stefano Pozzi has provided us with new inspiration and we are grateful for his thoughts on mathematical chaos. We would also like to thank Ann McDougal for her patience in helping us with the final layout of this book.

Finally our thanks to all the members of our families who have been receptive and encouraging whilst we worked on this book and in particular to Jill Harris, Andrew Sutherland, Joanna Sutherland, Ian Sutherland, and Maurice and José Healy.

Chapter 1 BACKGROUND

Introduction

Computers are becoming more accessible within mathematics classrooms and this makes it important to find good software to encourage pupils to explore and express mathematical ideas. We believe that spreadsheets offer this potential. Four years ago we committed ourselves to working with spreadsheets knowing very little about what pupils would be able to do with them. This work seems to have paid off and we are now continually finding new problems and related mathematical ideas which can be investigated within a spreadsheet environment.

This book is a record of our work over the last four years. By trying out materials both with pupils in the classroom and with teachers on in-service courses we have gradually modified the problems we use. By working closely with pupils we have begun to distinguish between the difficult aspects of spreadsheet use and how these interact with mathematical ideas. By refining the introductory problems the initial stages of spreadsheet work can be made more comprehensible to pupils, allowing them to exploit the full power of the environment more quickly. The problems presented are intended only as starting points because our ultimate aim is for teachers and pupils to make decisions themselves about which mathematical problems can usefully be solved with a spreadsheet environment.

It is becoming increasingly difficult to answer questions about which problems should be used with which aged pupils. We find 12-year-olds who can confidently work with problems which some 17-year-olds find difficult. Of one thing we are certain – once pupils can confidently use a spreadsheet then they will surprise you with the type of mathematical activities they tackle. It seems that the reason why so many pupils enjoy working in computer-based environments is that they offer intellectual challenges which are often missing in the standard mathematics curriculum.

What is a Spreadsheet?

A spreadsheet is like a big electronic table which is used for presenting and manipulating data (both text and numbers). In some senses a spreadsheet can be thought of as similar to a programming language. The advantage of spreadsheets over other programming environments is that pupils can use them to express and manipulate mathematical relationships without actually taking on board all the complexities of a formal language. Like all programming languages a spreadsheet is good for solving certain kinds of problems and not so good for solving others.

The Choice of a Spreadsheet Package

When we first started our work, we tried out a number of spreadsheet packages. At the same time we explored different approaches to teaching pupils how to use them. We came to the conclusion that EXCEL[1] was the most accessible for pupils of all ages. Although we do not wish to push a particular software package, all our work with computers suggests that the design of a computer environment, and in particular the way the learner has to interact with it, can crucially effect the understandings which the learner develops. We realise that as teachers you will have to use the package which is available in your school but suggest that you become aware of the advantages and disadvantages of this package and are prepared to respond to new developments.

The education world often designs software specifically for the classroom and this has been the case with spreadsheets. The aim of this purpose-built educational software is to restrict the computer environment and this often results in the pupils being restricted. Moreover because of limitations of funding, these educational packages usually do not offer the editing facilities which are available within more commercially produced software. The design of educational packages is often based on preconceived ideas about what pupils can and cannot do in non-computational environments, before anything is known about what pupils can and cannot do within the computer environment.

Our Approach to Teaching

Our approach to teaching has strongly influenced the way we have developed the spreadsheet problems presented in this book. The computer perturbs the normal role of the teacher. Pupils become very motivated and engaged in a problem and so seem to need less support. However, all our experience suggests that the teacher's role is crucial both in structuring the learning environment and in encouraging pupils to reflect on their problem-solving processes and the mathematical ideas being used. Part of the critical and most difficult aspect of being a teacher is to know when to leave pupils alone and when to intervene. It has been our experience that both too much intervention and a lack of intervention can have a negative effect on pupils' learning. For some years we have been recording our own interventions with pupils and have sometimes found them to be inappropriate. One of the most important aspects of being a teacher is to build up a good working relationship with pupils. When this happens, pupils are able to discuss and if necessary reject inappropriate suggestions. If this good relationship has not been established then pupils place too much emphasis on the teacher's suggestions and lose confidence in their own ability to solve problems. It is usually because of a fear of inappropriately intervening that teachers leave pupils to work on their own in computer environments. This can result in pupils losing their sense of direction and challenge and, more importantly, the potential for learning.

We have developed a number of guidelines which influence our continuing work in the classroom. Our primary aim is to develop a bank of good mathematical problems which confront pupils with the need to use and understand specific mathematical ideas. In order to minimise our interventions we aim for these problems to be:

[1] This is available for the RML Nimbus, IBM and Apple Macintosh computers.

- highly motivating,
- accessible to a wide range of pupils,
- extensible so that pupils can work productively at different rates,
- flexible enough to allow for a range of problem solving approaches.

When we do intervene we are influenced by a desire to:

- make clear the aims of the activity,
- encourage reflection on process,
- help pupils develop confidence in their own ability to solve mathematical problems,
- help pupils develop flexibility in their approach to problem solving,
- provide pupils with the syntax of the language,
- make suggestions related to the use of new mathematical ideas.

We have observed one type of behaviour when pupils are working at the computer which is almost always unproductive from the point of view of learning. This has been called working at a syntactical level (Hoyles & Sutherland, 1989) and in a spreadsheet environment might involve entering meaningless code without any reflection on the outcome of this code. Although in our earlier days of working with computers we were open-minded about this type of behaviour, we are now more likely to intervene to encourage pupils to reflect on the processes involved, because we have found working at a syntactical level to be unproductive both in terms of solving a particular task and in terms of learning mathematical ideas. We have also found that if pupils are encouraged to reflect on the meaning of the syntax from the beginning of their work with spreadsheets, then they are less likely to work at a superficially syntactical level.

The Mathematical Potential of a Spreadsheet

During our work with spreadsheets in the classroom, we have been able to observe which mathematical ideas pupils are using to solve particular problems. In our experience it is very difficult to distinguish between use and understanding of a mathematical idea. If pupils are using mathematical ideas in a reflective and meaningful way, then this is highly related to understanding. The most exciting aspect of the spreadsheet environment is that it allows pupils to express general mathematical relationships which are far more sophisticated than those which they can normally express in their paper and pencil work. This potential for expressing generalities is linked to the value of a spreadsheet environment from the point of view of developing algebraic understandings. Indeed, because of our own particular interests, many of the problems which are presented in this book are very closely related to the algebra curriculum. Throughout the book wherever we present a spreadsheet activity we describe both the spreadsheet and mathematical ideas which pupils are likely to use when solving the activity.

Overview of the Book

The book is organised around spreadsheet activities which can be photo-copied and are intended for use in the mathematics classroom. As well as describing the spreadsheet and mathematical ideas which pupils are likely to use when solving the problems, we present <u>Notes on Classroom Use</u> which are based on our observations from work with pupils and teachers. When appropriate, we have included short descriptions of pupils working on a particular activity to highlight potential issues which might arise when the activity is used in the classroom.

Pupils need to be able to use a spreadsheet effectively before they can begin to exploit the power of a spreadsheet to investigate and consolidate mathematical ideas. Chapter 2 deals with Getting Started and presents materials which introduce pupils to the following spreadsheet ideas:

- entering data: text, numbers and formulae,
- copying formulae containing relative references,
- presenting data.

Whereas Chapter 2 deals with the essential aspects of spreadsheet use, Chapter 3 presents materials which can be used to extend pupils' facility with a spreadsheet and in particular the following aspects of spreadsheets are dealt with:

- using a combination of absolute and relative references,
- naming a cell,
- using a conditional statement,
- plotting a range of graphs,
- sum, average and other spreadsheet functions.

Chapter 4 centres around the use of a spreadsheet to express and explore mathematical ideas. Problems related to the following ideas are presented:

- algebraic expressions,
- financial modelling,
- numerical solutions of equations,
- two ways of expressing a sequence,
- in the limit,
- optimisation problems,
- differences of equations,
- strange behaviour and chaos.

Chapter 5 presents an overview of the facilities of most spreadsheet packages, describing the significant differences between the currently available packages in schools. When necessary, translations between the syntax of these different packages is provided. All the illustrations in this book have used the spreadsheet EXCEL, although we have designed materials which are as far as possible spreadsheet-independent.

Chapter 6 consolidates and discusses the issues presented within the previous chapters making comments on the relationship between spreadsheet work and the National Curriculum.

Chapter 2 STARTING TO USE A SPREADSHEET

Introduction

Before pupils can begin to exploit the power of a spreadsheet to investigate and consolidate mathematical ideas, they need to be able to use the spreadsheet effectively and be aware of its potential. This chapter introduces activities which are concerned with the beginning stages of learning to use a spreadsheet. In devising introductory spreadsheet activities we aim to find a balance between prescriptive and open-ended activities. Pupils at this stage left in open-ended situations lack the knowledge to close the situation for themselves. Alternatively a very prescriptive sequence of activities is too constraining and can result in a decrease in motivation and engagement in the task. The focus of this book is mathematics and consequently all of the activities are concerned with learning mathematics as well as learning how to use a spreadsheet.

The essential aspects of the spreadsheet which pupils need to learn are:

- entering data: text, numbers and formulae,
- copying formulae using relative referencing,
- presentation of data.

This chapter consists of a collection of introductory activities. Alongside each activity presented in this chapter we list both the spreadsheet and mathematical ideas which we predict pupils will use when working on the activity. We provide some notes for the teacher, describing issues which have arisen from trying out the activities in the classroom. Occasionally we add an illustrative episode. We have had, by necessity, to present activities in a sequence but this sequence is not intended to be rigidly adhered to.

Once pupils are confident in defining formulae and can understand the way in which these formulae can be constructed from values or rules in other cells and can copy them using relative referencing; they will then be equipped with the necessary tools to attempt a variety of mathematical problem-solving activities in a spreadsheet environment.

Entering Data and Formulae

A spreadsheet is rather like a big electronic table. It consists of a number of cells arranged in rows and columns. The labelling of these rows and columns varies according to the spreadsheet package although there are two main ways of doing this. Throughout this book we will use the convention shown in Fig. 2.1, where A, B, C etc are used to label columns and 1, 2, 3 etc are used to label rows. Other conventions are discussed in Chapter 5. Three types of data can be entered into a cell of a spreadsheet. These are:

- text
- numbers
- formulae

We want pupils to learn to enter formulae at the beginning stages of spreadsheet use and consequently have prepared activities which confront pupils with the need to enter numbers and formulae simultaneously.

	A	B	C	D	
1					
2					
3					
4					
5					
6					
7					
8					
9					

Fig 2.1: A Spreadsheet table.

The time that pupils will need to spend on the following activities varies considerably between pupils. If pupils are not given enough time to experiment with entering and reflecting on formulae, then the subsequent introduction of replicating these formulae may not be well understood. Conversely, spending too much time before introducing the replicating feature of the spreadsheet may leave pupils unaware of the spreadsheet's potential as a problem-solving tool.

Find the Formula (Activity 2.1)

Pupils are given the Find the Formula activity and shown how to enter a number in one cell and a formula related to this number in another cell. In carrying out this activity pupils are likely to confront the following spreadsheet and mathematical ideas:

Spreadsheet ideas	Mathematical ideas
Convention of labelling cells.	Use of brackets.
Entering of numbers into cells.	Use of arithmetical operations.
Entering of formulae into cells.	Order of operations.
Familiarisation of layout.	Identity of expressions.
	Use of decimal numbers.
	Symbolic expression of functions.
	Conjecturing.

	A	B	C
1			
2			
3		6	
4			
5			
6			
7			

Without letting your partner see what you are doing, enter a number into a cell.

In another cell enter a formula which does something to this number.

	A	B	C
1			
2			
3			6
4			=B3+3
5			
6			
7			

This formula takes the number in cell B3 and adds 3 to it.

Your partner must try to work out your formula.

	A	B	C
1			
2			
3		6	
4			9
5			
6			
7			

Your partner can only change this number.

Check the idea by entering it as a formula and comparing the results.

• The teacher's role is very important in showing pupils how to enter a formula into the spreadsheet. Pupils should do this for themselves with the teacher being available both for support and to tell pupils the critical aspects of the spreadsheet syntax (e.g. use of = sign to enter formulae).

• Pupils should be encouraged to enter data into cells anywhere on the spreadsheet. In doing this they can explore the extent of the spreadsheet and learn how to move around it becoming familiar with the spreadsheet layout.

• A common difficulty which pupils experience when beginning to define formulae is that they forget to include the unknown in their formula. So for example they might enter data as shown in Fig 2.2. However, unlike the paper and pencil algebra context, pupils gain feedback from the computer which provokes them to reflect on their error.

	A	B
1	7	
2		
3		=*5
4		
5		
6		

Fig. 2.2: Incorrect use of spreadsheet notation.

The following examples illustrate some of the ways in which this activity has been used.

The equivalence of two algebraic expressions. Gary and Mike are two 13-year-olds and on their first spreadsheet session Gary entered the formula shown in Fig 2.3.

	A	B	C
1			
2		3	
3			
4			
5			
6			=B2+10*5
7			
8			

Fig. 2.3: Gary's formula.

After trying out several numbers in cell B2 Mike correctly decided that Gary's formula was 'plus 50'. Gary's response was to say that Mike was wrong, giving as a reason that his formula did 'two things'. But Mike was convinced that he was correct. He tried some more examples using the computer feedback to support his conjecture. Gary persisted in saying that it was not the same because his formula did 'two things'.

At this stage the boys could not resolve their disagreement. So the teacher suggested that Mike enter his predicted formula into the spreadsheet to see if both formulae always gave the same result. They did this and, after repeatedly changing the number in cell B2, Gary became convinced that both formulae produced the same result. However, he was still insistent that it was not the same formula because he knew that his formula did 'two things'. Eventually, Gary revealed his formula, and together the boys attempted to make sense of what was happening. Mike quickly realised that the 50 came from 5 times 10. The spreadsheet task had provoked them into reflecting on the equivalence of two algebraic/arithmetic expressions.

Chronis and Panos had a similar experience. Panos defined a formula as shown in Fig 2.4 saying that he had done 'two things'.

	A	B	C
1			
2			
3	5		
4			
5			
6			
7	=A3+2*15		
8			

Fig. 2.4: Panos' formula.

After trying out certain cases, Chronis was convinced that he had found Panos' formula and entered the formula shown on cell C5 of Fig 2.5. They found that both formulae produced the same output for the same input. Panos was not convinced that they were the same until Chronis explained:

'It's always plus 30, but you said two things, so I done 5 times 6 is 30, could be 3 times 10, it's always the same'.

	A	B	C
1			
2			
3	5		
4			
5			=A3+5*6
6			
7	35		
8			

Fig. 2.5: Chronis' prediction.

Devising a strategy for guessing any rule: Kevin and Andrea used the <u>Find the Formula</u> activity to develop a strategy for being able to work out any rule involving only one operation (e.g. y + 6.3). Kevin worked out that if he entered the number zero into the rule he could then work out if the operation was either addition or subtraction. If it involved addition or subtraction, he was confident that he would be ready to predict Andrea's formula. If it was not addition or subtraction he would then enter the number 1, and suggest that the formula was the number in the cell multiplied by the result of operating on 1. This led to some interesting discussions when his partner's formula included division, with Kevin arguing that multiplying by 0.35714285 is the same as dividing by 2.8 (Andrea's formula).

Undoing a Formula (Activity 2.2)

The activity <u>Undoing a Formula</u> (Activity 2.2) is an extension of <u>Find the Formula</u>. Some pupils spend considerable time on the first activity whereas other pupils need alternative activities, which also help to consolidate their understanding of constructing formulae. In carrying out this activity pupils are likely to use the following ideas:

Spreadsheet ideas	Mathematical ideas
Convention of labelling cells.	Use of brackets.
Entering of numbers into cells.	Use of arithmetical operations.
Entering of formulae into cells.	Order of arithmetical operations.
Familiarisation of layout.	Decimal numbers.
Referencing a cell which contains a formula.	Identity of expressions.
	Function and inverse function.
	Conjecturing.

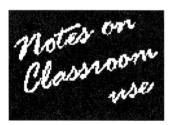

• This activity particularly encourages pupils to reflect on the order in which calculations are performed within the formulae they construct.

• We found that this activity provoked some children to use brackets, and provided an appropriate opportunity for teachers to introduce this idea. This is illustrated by the following example.

The need for brackets: Simone and Adeola were working on <u>Undoing a Formula.</u> They had previously explored the <u>Find the Formula</u> activity, but neither of them had ever used brackets within any of the formulae they had constructed. Adeola had defined the formula shown in Fig. 2.6.

Enter a starting number in one cell and
a formula which uses this number in
another cell.

For example:

	A	B	C
1			
2	3		
3		= A2 + 7	
4			
5			
6			
7			

Your partner must first try to
work out your formula and
then enter a formula to
UNDO your formula.

	A	B	C
1			
2	3		
3		10	
4			
5		=B3-7	
6			
7			

Change the starting number a few times
to check the second formula always
UNDOES the first.

	A	B	C
1			
2	3		
3		10	
4			
5		3	
6			
7			

	A	B	C
1			
2	25		
3		32	
4			
5		25	
6			
7			

	A	B	C
1		number	
2		27	
3	formula		
4	=B2/3+1		
5			
6			
7			
8			

Fig. 2.6: Adeola's Formula.

	A	B	C
1		number	
2		27	
3	formula		
4	=B2/3+1		undo form
5			=A4-1*3
6			
7			
8			

Fig. 2.7: Undoing the formula: omission of brackets.

After considerable exploration, and some help from her partner, Simone worked out this relationship. She entered the formula shown in cell C5 on fig 2.7, which she was convinced would undo Adeola's formula. They were both extremely surprised when instead of the expected 27 this formula produced 7.

Simone was still convinced that she had correctly defined the inverse function. She cleared the formula and tried the same again. The formula still produced 7. At this point she asked for help:

'10 minus 1 is 9 times 3 is 27, but it keeps saying 7, look'.

After discussing this with the teacher, Simone defined the formula using brackets (see Fig 2.8).

The computer feedback had confronted Simone with the need to match the syntax of the spreadsheet's algebraic formulation with the rule which Simone quite clearly understood.

	A	B	C
1		number	
2		27	
3	formula		
4	=B2/3+1		undo form
5			=(A4-1)*3
6			
7			
8			

Fig. 2.8: Undoing the formula: using brackets.

Copying Formulae containing Relative References

The activities included in this section are all concerned with replicating rules containing relative references. There is overlap between these activities and some pupils will pick up the ideas involved very quickly. Nevertheless at this stage it is important that pupils have the opportunity to focus on the replication of a variety of formulae, including those containing more than one cell reference, otherwise they may develop a restricted view of the possibilities within a spreadsheet environment.

Generating the Natural Numbers (Activity 2.3)

Pupils are asked to replicate a formula in order to produce the natural numbers on a spreadsheet. In carrying out this activity pupils are likely to use the following spreadsheet and mathematical ideas.

Spreadsheet ideas	Mathematical ideas
Entering of formulae.	Generation of arithmetical sequences.
Replication of formulae containing relative references.	Use of symbolic notation to express arithmetic sequences.

When a rule containing a **relative reference** is copied, the physical relationship between the cell containing the referenced cell will be preserved. Fig. 2.9b shows what happens when the formula "**=A1 + 1** " contained in cell A2, is copied down into the cells below it. This formula generates the sequence of natural numbers shown in Fig 2.9a.

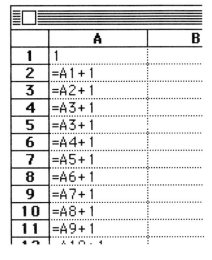

	A	B
1	1	
2	2	
3	3	
4	4	
5	5	
6	6	
7	7	
8	8	
9	9	
10	10	
11	11	

	A	B
1	1	
2	=A1+1	
3	=A2+1	
4	=A3+1	
5	=A3+1	
6	=A4+1	
7	=A5+1	
8	=A6+1	
9	=A7+1	
10	=A8+1	
11	=A9+1	

Fig. 2.9: Replicating a formula to generate the natural numbers.

• The language used by the teacher seems to be important in helping pupils to develop a framework for the idea of replication. For example, as a pupil was entering a rule of the form "**A1+1**" this would be be referred to as:

'take the number from the cell above and add 1'
or
'number above add 1'

This use of language encouraged pupils to focus on the 'generic' nature of the rule as opposed to the specific formula which was being entered.

GENERATING THE
NATURAL NUMBERS

Enter the number 1 into a cell, then enter
a formula in the cell directly underneath,
which adds 1 to this number.

	A	B	C
1			
2			
3			1
4		=B3+1	
5			
6			
7			
8			
9			
10			
11			

This formula
takes the
number in
the cell
above and
adds 1 to it.

Now copy this formula down into
the cells below.

	A	B	C
1			
2			
3		1	
4		2	
5		3	
6		4	
7		5	
8		6	
9		7	
10		8	
11		9	

Have a look in some of the
cells to see what happened to
the formula that you copied.

Change the starting number -
what happens?

• We found that the teacher had a very important role at this point, in encouraging pupils to reflect on, and make sense of, what was happening to a rule when it was replicated relatively. (For example, by suggesting that pupils try a range of different starting values for their replicated rule and attempt to predict the outcome of such a change.)

Generating Sequences (Activity 2.4)

Both this activity and Activity 2.5 are concerned with the generation of sequences. In carrying out <u>Generating Sequences</u> pupils are likely to use the following spreadsheet and mathematical ideas:

Spreadsheet ideas	Mathematical ideas
Entering of formulae.	Determining possible rules for generating a sequence.
Replication of formula containing relative references.	Use of symbolic notation to express sequences.

• We found that it was useful to encourage pupils to write down on paper the rules that they had used in generating the sequences in a way that represented the relative nature of these rules. We found this helped them to focus on the 'generic' nature of the rule as opposed to the specific formula which was being entered. This is illustrated by the following examples.

Writing down a rule: Richard and Sunil found that the formula shown in Fig 2.10 generated the square number sequence. They wrote this down on paper as:

> Square No. before + Previous pos + pos

Adeola and Simone defined a different formula which also generated the square number sequence (see Fig 2.11). They wrote down:

> Square numbers = Pos in Seq x itself

Can you enter formulae to generate the
first 20 terms of the following
sequences?

position in seq	odd numbers
1	1
2	3
3	5
4	7

position in seq	even numbers
1	2
2	4
3	6
4	8

position in seq	sequence
1	1
2	1
3	2
4	3
5	5
6	8
7	13

position in seq	sequence
1	1
2	3
3	4
4	7
5	11
6	18
7	29

How may different formulae can you find which will
generate the square number sequence?

position in seq	square nos.
1	1
2	4
3	9
4	16
5	25
6	36
7	49
8	64
9	81
10	100

	A	B	
1			
2			
3	position in seq	square no.	
4	1	1	
5	2	=B4+A4+A5	
6	3		
7	4		
8	5		
9	6		
10	7		
11	8		

Fig 2.10: Generating square numbers:
Richard and Sunil.

	A	B	
1			
2			
3	position in seq	square no.	
4	1	=A4*A4	
5	2		
6	3		
7	4		
8	5		
9	6		
10	7		
11	8		

Fig 2.11: Generating square numbers:
Adeola and Simone.

- At this stage some pupils started to extend the task for themselves by investigating the production of other sequences. For example some pupils wanted to construct a multiplication table, other pupils just seemed to want to take time out to *'see what happens if I do this'*.

Find the Sequence (Activity 2.5)

This activity is an extension of the activities Find the Formula and Undoing a Formula, the difference being that the sequence provides pupils with a table of numbers on which to base their conjectures. In carrying out this task pupils are likely to use the following spreadsheet and mathematical ideas.

Spreadsheet ideas	Mathematical ideas
Entering of formulae.	Generation of sequences.
Replication of formula containing relative references.	Use of symbolic notation to express sequences.
	Use of brackets.
	Use of arithmetical operations.
	Identity of formulae.
	Inverse functions.
	Conjecturing.

18

	A	B	C
1	position in seq	my sequence	
2	1	=A2*2.1	
3	2		
4	3		
5	4		
6	5		
7	6		
8	7		
9	8		
10	9		
11	10		
12	11		
13			

Generate the sequence of natural numbers starting with 1.

Without letting your partner see what you are doing, enter a formula which uses this 1 and copy it down the spreadsheet.

Your partner must try to work out a formula which generates your sequence.

Enter a formula and copy it down to check that the same sequence is produced.

	A	B	C
1	position in seq	my sequence	your sequence
2	1	2.1	
3	2	4.2	
4	3	6.3	
5	4	8.4	
6	5	10.5	
7	6	12.6	
8	7	14.7	
9	8	16.8	
10	9	18.9	
11	10	21	
12	11	23.1	
13			

Can you enter a formula which UNDOES the sequence?

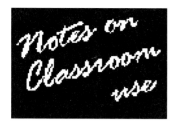

- Copying formulae which pupils have constructed for themselves motivates pupils to make sense of the replication process.

- Initially pupils tend to produce linear functions. In this case when a sequence is generated from the function there is a common difference between each term. They could use this common difference to generate the sequence with a recurrence relationship, but they tend to look for a universal rule because they know that this is what their partner was likely to have used. This is illustrated by the following example.

Using the recurrence relationship to discover the universal rule: Alice and Joanna were working together. Alice had defined and copied the formula shown in Fig. 2.12a below.

Joanna was attempting to find this formula and she noticed that the common difference was 4. She realised that she would be able to reproduce the sequence using a recurrence relation by adding 4 to the previous number in the sequence. She also knew that this would not give her Alice's formula because it had been defined as a universal rule. She focused on the common difference of 4 and after some experimentation worked out that Alice's formula involved multiplying by 4 and adding 8 (Fig. 2.12b). After this they continued to use this 'common difference' strategy to find the universal rule for any given linear function.

	A	B
1	1	=A1*4+8
2	2	
3	3	
4	4	
5	5	
6	6	
7	7	
8	8	
∩	∩	

Fig. 2.12a: A universal rule (formula)

	A	B
1	1	12
2	2	16
3	3	20
4	4	24
5	5	28
6	6	32
7	7	36
8	8	40
∩	∩	44

Fig. 2.12b: A universal rule (sequence)

- Pupils who find all the previous activities fairly straightforward are able to set each other more challenging problems. This is illustrated by the following example.

A more difficult problem: Andrew and Ardash had worked quickly through the previous activities. They used the <u>Find the Sequence</u> activity to devise a challenging problem for themselves. Ardash defined a formula which produced the sequence shown in Fig. 2.13.

	A	B	
1			
2	1	2	
3	2	6	
4	3	12	
5	4	20	
6	5	30	
7	6	42	
8	7	56	
9	8	72	
10	9	90	
11	10	110	
12	11	132	

Fig. 2.13: Ardash's sequence.

In order to work out the sequence Andrew tried out a number of linear relationships in his head. He then had the idea of generating the square numbers. After he had done this, he examined the difference between corresponding terms of Ardash's sequence and the square numbers. He worked out that this difference increased by 1 each time (Fig 2.14). This enabled him to devise a rule (*'number squared plus itself'*) to generate the given sequence.

	A	B	C	D
1				
2	1	2	1	=(A2*A2)+A2
3	2	6	4	
4	3	12	9	
5	4	20	16	
6	5	30	25	
7	6	42	36	
8	7	56	49	
9	8	72	64	
10	9	90	81	
11	10	110	100	
12	11	132	121	

Fig. 2.14: Andrew's final formula.

Presentation of Data

Within this section we present a problem which focuses more on the presentation aspects of a spreadsheet than on the use of mathematical ideas. This activity can also be used as an introductory spreadsheet problem. It is less open-ended than the Find the Formula activity and it more closely resembles the type of activity for which spreadsheets are used in the business world.

Ordering Clothes (Activity 2.6)

In carrying out Activity 2.6, pupils are likely to use the following spreadsheet and mathematical ideas.

Spreadsheet ideas	Mathematical ideas
Displaying and formatting data.	Decimal places.
Entering text as labels.	Multiplication.
Inserting blank rows and columns.	Percentages.
Entering of formulae related to two cells.	Choice and constraints.
Replication of formulae containing relative references.	Trial and error improvement methods.
The SUM function.	

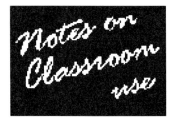

• When pupils solve this problem they usually want to display the information carefully and this provides an opportunity for showing them how data in cells can be formatted, including ideas such as the number of decimal places to use. It is also an opportunity to introduce pupils to how to insert blank rows and columns in a spreadsheet table.

• After pupils have worked out and entered the cost for several items of school uniform they are likely to ask questions like *'Do we have to keep on entering the same rule'*, and this provides an opportunity for introducing the idea of replicating formulae.

• Pupils will tend to ask if there is an 'easy way' of entering the rule for the 'Total Cost'. This provides an opportunity for introducing the SUM function as illustrated in Fig 2.15.

	A	B	C	D	
1	ITEM	UNIT COST	NUMBER	COST	
2	Shirts	8.99	2	=B2*C2	
3	T-Shirts (PE)	3.99	3	=B3*C3	
4	Skirts	15.49	0	=B4*C4	
5	Trousers	21	1	=B5*C5	
6	Shorts (PE)	4.99	2	=B6*C6	
7	Socks (PE)	1.49	4	=B7*C7	
8					
9			TOTAL	=SUM(D2:D7)	
10					

Fig. 2.15: Using the SUM function.

Use a spreadsheet to calculate the cost of
school uniform.

	A	B	C	D	E
1	ITEM	UNIT COST	NUMBER	COST	
2	Shirts	8.99			
3	T-Shirts (PE)	3.99			
4	Skirts	15.49			
5	Trousers	21.00			
6	Shorts (PE)	4.99			
7	Socks (PE)	1.49			
8					
9			TOTAL		

In this cell, enter a formula which calculates cost by multiplying unit cost by number of items. Copy this into the cells below.

In this cell, enter a formula which calculates the total cost.

- Use this spreadsheet to work out the total cost for the following orders:

  a) 2 shirts, 3 T-shirts, 1 skirt, 1 pair of trousers, 2 pairs of shorts and 4 pairs of socks.

  b) 5 shirts, 2 T-shirts, 3 skirts, 2 pairs of trousers and 6 pairs of socks.

- You have £75.00 to spend on your school uniform. You must buy at least 1 shirt, 1 T-shirt, 1 pair of trousers, 1 pair of shorts and one pair of socks. Use the spreadsheet to work out all the different ways you could spend your £75.00.

- You have just heard that all the prices have increased by 8%. How would this affect your answers to the above questions?

• The question about spending £75 introduces the idea of choice and constraints within mathematical problem-solving. The spreadsheet allows pupils to use a trial and error approach after they have specified the constraints of the problem.

• Pupils can devise their own related problems (e.g. organising a school party) which can involve a more practical activity.

Systematic trial and error: Alison and Heidi, two 14-year-old pupils, tried out this problem during their second spreadsheet session. They initially asked for help in order to widen the columns so that 'T-Shirts(PE)' would all appear in the cell. They again needed support when they entered the formula to calculate the total cost of an item (see Fig. 2.15) but after being told how to do this for 'Shirts' were able to enter the formulae themselves for the cost of the other items. In order to answer the question about the different ways of spending £75 they developed a systematic trial and error approach, first using the spreadsheet to work out that 'essential costs' came to £36.47 and then recording their results on paper as shown in Fig 2.16 below.

They then avoided doing any mathematical calculations to answer the last question 'You have just heard that all the prices have increased by 8%. How would this affect your answers to the above questions?'
by writing down *'Less clothes would be able to be bought'.* In the following lesson Alison and Heidi were asked to refine their answer by using the spreadsheet to calculate the percentage increases and work out the new possibilities for spending £75.

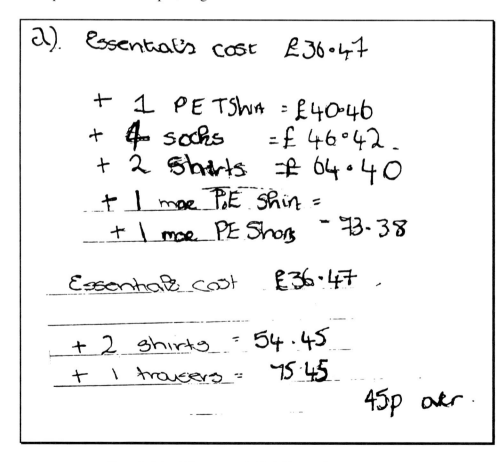

Fig. 2.16: Alison and Heidi's written record.

24

Chapter 3 EXTENDING SPREADSHEET USE

Introduction

Whereas Chapter 2 deals with the essential aspects of spreadsheet use this chapter will present materials which can be used to extend pupils' facility with a spreadsheet package. Pupils should be confident with the ideas presented in Chapter 2 before they work on the following ideas which are the focus of this chapter.

- Using a combination of absolute and relative referencing,
- Using a conditional statement,
- Plotting a range of graphs,
- Sum, average and other spreadsheet functions.

Using a Combination of Absolute and Relative Referencing

You may sometimes wish to refer to a particular rule in a spreadsheet cell, without wanting this rule to change in a relative way when it is copied into other spreadsheet cells. Under these circumstances you can enter a formula containing an absolute reference. In most spreadsheet packages it is possible to do this by giving a cell a name. This name[1] will always refer to the contents of the named cell. We present below two problems which we have found to be valuable when introducing this idea to pupils.

Generating Arithmetic Sequences (Activity 3.1)

In this problem pupils are first asked to generate the sequence of positive odd numbers. In order to do this they are asked to name the 'first' term and the 'difference' between terms. Naming these variables will allow any arithmetic sequence to be generated with the same general formula, once the first term and the difference between terms have been given specific values. In carrying out this activity pupils are likely to use the spreadsheet and mathematical ideas shown on page 27.

---

[1] We chose to use this method of absolute referencing because we found it to be less confusing for pupils than using the notation for absolute cell referencing. This issue is discussed more fully in Chapter 5.

GENERATING ARITHMETIC SEQUENCES

By naming cells you can use the same spreadsheet to generate many different sequences

Name this cell first

Name this cell difference

	A	B	C	D
1				
2		1	2	
3				
4		=first		
5		=B4+difference		
6		=B5+difference		
7		=B6+difference		
8		=B7+difference		
9		=B8+difference		
10		=B9+difference		

This formula takes the number from the cell named **first**

This formula adds the number in the cell named **difference** to the number in the cell above

This spreadsheet generates the following arithmetic sequence

	A	B	C	D
1				
2		1	2	
3				
4		1		
5		3		
6		5		
7		7		
8		9		
9		11		
10		13		

Now use this spreadsheet to generate the following arithmetic sequences

1.0	15	-40
2.5	13	-43
4.0	11	-46
5.5	9	-49
7.0	7	-52
...	...	...
...	...	...
...	...	...

Spreadsheet ideas	Mathematical ideas
Naming a cell.	Decimal and negative numbers.
Differences between the name and the contents of a cell.	Variable.
Differences between relative and absolute references.	Use of symbolic notation to express an arithmetic sequence.
Replicating a formula containing absolute references.	Importance of first term and common difference in generating an arithmetic sequence.

• The teacher's role is important in showing pupils that the named cell (absolute reference) does not change when the rule is replicated.

• It is a good idea to let pupils choose the names themselves encouraging a range of nonsense, meaningful and single letter names so that pupils realise that any name can be used.

• It is important to help pupils differentiate between naming a cell and entering text data. The name of the cell is invisible to the user but we have found that pupils usually know which cell they have named.

• It is useful to use the GOTO command (when this is available in the spreadsheet package) to find the named cell (e.g. GOTO difference).

• We have deliberately included sequences which use both decimal and negative numbers so that pupils' understanding of arithmetic sequences is not restricted to positive whole numbers. The spreadsheet environment is particularly valuable in this respect.

Arithmetic and Geometric Sequences (Activity 3.2)

This activity is an extension of Generating Arithmetic Sequences and provides another situation for naming a cell as an absolute reference. When carrying out this activity pupils are likely to use the spreadsheet and mathematical ideas shown on page 28.

Spreadsheet Ideas	Mathematical Ideas
Naming a cell.	Decimal and negative numbers.
Differences between relative and absolute reference.	Variable.
Differences between the name and contents of a cell.	Use of symbolic notation to express arithmetic and geometric sequences.
Replicating formulae containing absolute references.	Importance of the first term and common difference in generating an arithmetic sequence.
	Importance of the first term and common ratio in generating a geometric sequence.
	The power of symbolism to express generality.

• The teacher's role is important in encouraging pupils to enter a general formula to generate any arithmetic sequence otherwise pupils will tend to enter a new formula for each specific arithmetic sequence presented on the worksheet. The same applies to the formula for geometric sequences.

• We have tried out this activity both with 12-year-old pupils who had no previous experience of arithmetic and geometric sequences and with 17-year-old pupils who had used the ideas within their A-level mathematics course.

Noticing generality: Susie and Zoe are two quiet but mathematically confident 12-year-olds. They had previously used a spreadsheet to enter and relatively copy formulae containing relative references and before working on this activity were introduced to <u>Generating Arithmetic Sequences</u>. They successfully used a combination of absolute and relative references to generate the sequence, 2, 34, 66, 98, 130.....

When they started to generate the next sequence on the worksheet they moved to another part of the spreadsheet and started again to enter the formulae containing a combination of absolute and relative references. They had not seen that their original formula was general enough to enable them to enter all the arithmetic sequences. This was also the same for the A-level pupils when they worked on this activity. Another approach would be to ask the pupils to generate all the sequences on the worksheet and then introduce them to the idea of referencing and absolute referencing when they themselves perceived the generality and demanded *'an easier way to solve the problem'*.

When Susie and Zoe worked on the geometric sequences they were able to work out the first sequence (1, 2, 4, 8..) without any difficulty. In the spreadsheet environment this geometric sequence was no more difficult for

Identify the differences and the similarities in the 4 arithmetic sequences

Can you enter ONE formula that can generate all the sequences?

2	7.0	-72	-0.64
34	6.8	-65	-0.32
66	6.6	-58	0.00
98	6.4	-51	0.32
130	6.2	-44	0.64
162	6.0	-37	0.96
194	5.8	-30	1.28
226	5.6	-23	1.60
...	...	...	...
...	...	...	...
...	...	...	...

Do the same for these geometric sequences

1	3.1	6	32
2	9.3	-6	-16
4	27.9	6	8
8	83.7	-6	-4
16	251.1	6	2
32	753.3	-6	-1
64	2259.9	6	0.5
...	...	...	...
...	...	...	...
...	...	...	...
...	...	...	...

them to generate than the previous arithmetic sequence. The third sequence (6, -6, 6 , -6...) did present them with difficulties because they immediately thought that the rule should be 'minus, add, minus, add' . The constraint of using the same rule which they had used for the previous geometric sequences eventually led them to realise that multiplying by minus 1 would be a solution. This problem presented Susie and Zoe with ideas which they had not formally met within their mathematics curriculum. The activity was one of investigation which could then at a later stage provide a basis for more formal links with standard algebraic notation.

Linking spreadsheet and algebra formalisms: Adele and Pat are two A-level pupils who because of their previous experiences of A-level mathematics had no difficulties in seeing the mathematical relationships within the sequences and the activity for them was less rich in terms of investigation of mathematical ideas. It was nevertheless important in helping them make links between their previously learned mathematical formalisms and the spreadsheet formalisms for generating arithmetic and geometric sequences. So, for example, the algebraic notation for the recurrence relation for generating a geometric sequence is:

$$g_1 = a$$

$$g_n = r g_{n-1}$$

where:-

$a =$ the first term of the geometric sequence

$r =$ the ratio between consecutive terms

$g_n =$ the nth term of the geometric sequence

and this can be compared with the spreadsheet formalism presented in Fig. 3.1.

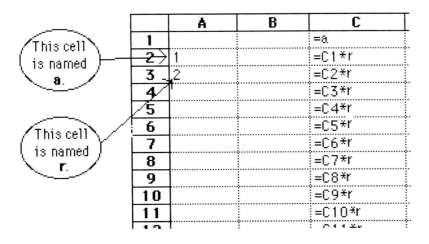

Fig. 3.1: Spreadsheet formalism to generate a geometric progression.

Using a Conditional Statement

For most spreadsheet packages it is possible to enter a conditional expression into a spreadsheet cell as illustrated in Fig. 3.2.

	A	B	C	
1				
2				
3	4		=IF(A3<20,A3+5,2*A3)	
4				
5				
6				
7				

Fig. 3.2: A conditional statement.

It is difficult to find introductory spreadsheet problems in which a conditional statement is used in a non-trivial way. In our experience when pupils need the idea they can begin to use it effectively, although they will not necessarily confront all the implications of the different logical combinations of an expression. We have devised two introductory problems. The first (Record Shop Prices) provides a more routine introduction to the idea and the second (Guess the Inequality) can be used in a more investigational way.

Record Shop Prices (Activity 3.3)

Activity 3.3 introduces pupils to the following spreadsheet and mathematical ideas:

Spreadsheet Ideas	Mathematical Ideas
Conditional formulae. Replication of formulae using relative referencing.	Decimal and negative numbers. Variable. Formalising inequalities. Equivalent logical combinations of conditional expressions.

31

Use a spreadsheet to show the cost of items in a record shop in 1990

	A	B	C	D
1		1990	1991	
2	ITEM	UNIT COST	UNIT COST	
3	COMPACT DISC	11.99	=IF(B3<8,B3+0.50,B3)	
4	LP RECORD	7.99		
5	SINGLES	1.99		
6	12 INCH	3.99		
7	TAPES	8.49		
8				
9				

If the number in B3 is less than 8, then add 0.50 to it, otherwise it stays the same.

In 1991, new prices were calculated according to the following rule:

If the 1990 price was less than £8.00 then it increased by 50p in 1991.
Items over £8.00 stayed the same.

In 1992 prices increased again. This time items costing over £8.00 in 1991 increased by 99p, and items costing less than £8.00 in 1991 increased by 49p.

Enter a rule on your spreadsheet to calculate the 1992 prices.

How much more would it cost to buy one of each item in 1992 compared to 1990?

• Teachers will need to provide considerable support with syntax at the beginning of this activity.

Starting to use conditional expressions: Eleanor and Joanne are two quiet but mathematically confident 12-year-old pupils who tried out this problem. They were able to calculate the 1991 unit costs from the instructions on the worksheet before entering the rule into the spreadsheet. This was important because it meant that they could make sense of the values generated by the spreadsheet rules. The spreadsheet syntax matched their own problem solutions but they still had difficulty in remembering the precise nature of the syntax in order to enter their own rules. They were more confident when they entered the rule for the 1992 record prices and at this point asked if they could copy the conditional formula into the 1992 column. In this sense they seemed to have seen the generality of the conditional expression.

Guess the Inequality (Activity 3.4)

Activity 3.4 allows for more mathematical investigation than Activity 3.3 and for some pupils is more motivating, although for others it may present a too open-ended introduction to inequalities. The mathematical ideas used could be more extensive than those used in the previous problem, and include the following.

Spreadsheet Idea	Mathematical Ideas
Conditional formulae.	Formalising inequalities. Equivalent logical combinations of conditional expressions. Decimal and negative numbers. Continuity of decimal numbers. Conjecturing. The role of a counter example.

This activity is very similar to Find the Formula (Activity 2.1) except that in this case pupils have to work out an inequality expression which their partner has formalised.

Enter a number into a cell on your spreadsheet.

	A	B
1		
2	13	
3		
4		
5		
6		
7		
8		
9		

In another cell enter a formula

	A	B
1		
2	13	
3		
4		
5		
6		=IF(A2<15,A2+10,A2-10)
7		
8		
9		

If the number in A2 is less than 15, then add 10 to it, otherwise subtract 10 from it.

	A	B
1		
2	13	
3		
4		
5		
6		23
7		
8		
9		

	A	B
1		
2	17	
3		
4		
5		
6		7
7		
8		
9		

Your partner must now try and work out your inequality and check the idea by entering it as a formula and comparing the results.

Equivalence of inequalities: Eleanor and Joanne, who had previously worked on <u>Record Shop Prices</u> (Activity 3.2) immediately became involved in this problem. Eleanor first wanted to enter a formula to represent *'If under 17 take away 14. If over 17 add 21'*. She needed help to express this formally in the spreadsheet (Fig. 3.3).

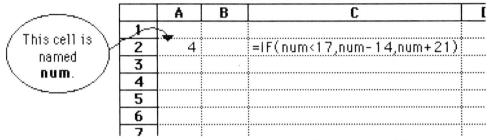

Fig. 3.3: If under 17 take away 14. If over 17 add 2.

By entering numbers in the cell A2 Joanne was able to predict the formula correctly and wrote down on paper:

If under 17 – 14 if over then + 24.

Eleanor then entered the following formula *'If over 20 then add 12, otherwise take away 0'* (Fig. 3.4).

	A	B	C	D
1				
2	13		=IF(num>20,num+12,num)	
3				
4				
5				
6				
7				

Fig. 3.4: If over 20, add 12, otherwise take away 0.

After trying out a range of positive whole numbers Joanne correctly predicted the formula.

After a nudge from the teacher Joanne next entered the formula to express *'If over 6.5 multiply by 3, otherwise divide by 2'*.

	A	B	C	[
1				
2	7.2		=IF(num>6.5,num*3,num/2)	
3				
4				
5				
6				
7				

Fig. 3.5: If over 6.5 multiply by 3, otherwise divide by 2.

By working on the previous examples Eleanor knew that she needed to find the precise number at which the inequality function changes. She did not have any difficulty in working out that the two rules used were 'multiply by 3 and divide by 2'. She started to enter decimal numbers between 6 and 7 and knew that when for example 6.4 was entered the number obtained (3.2) resulted from dividing by 2. She next tried 6.55 and when 19.65 was produced became confused because she knew that this was not divide by 2. After more trial and error she decided that the rule was: *If under 6.51 divide by 2. If over 6.51 multiply by 3.* She then entered a formula into the spreadsheet (as shown in Fig. 3.6).

	A	B	C	[
1				
2	6.52		=IF(num>6.51,num*3,num/2)	
3				
4				
5			=IF(num<6.51,num/2,num*3)	
6				
7				

Fig. 3.6: Eleanor's incorrect formula.

She tried out a range of numbers and was still convinced that the formulae were identical. Joanne however knew that both inequalities were not identical. At this point the teacher suggested that Joanne should enter a number (a counter example) which would demonstrate to Eleanor that the two inequalities were not identical. She entered 6.502 (Fig. 3.7).

	A	B	C	[
1				
2	6.502		19.506	
3				
4			3.251	
5				
6				
7				

Fig. 3.7: A counter example.

More discussion ensued. Joanne, who had never been formally introduced to formalising inequalities in her mathematics lesson, demonstrated a remarkable understanding and Eleanor was at least convinced that both formulae did not produce identical values for all numbers. This activity has so many potential extensions. At the beginning there had been a need for considerable support from the teacher, particularly with respect to the nudge about using decimals and the role of a counter example but eventually the pupils by their collaboration and interaction with the computer were testing out their mathematical conjectures. Both Joanne and Eleanor said that they had enjoyed this activity more than the Record Shop Prices Activity because it had involved more *'hard thinking'*.

Graph Plotting

Graphing facilities are available within certain spreadsheet packages although they are not always easy to use in ways which support mathematics learning (see Chapter 5 for more details).

Plotting a Range of Graphs (Activity 3.5)

We used Activity 3.5 to introduce pupils to the idea of using and investigating the graphical representation of sequences generated by a range of formulae. In carrying out this activity pupils are likely to use the following mathematical ideas.

Spreadsheet Ideas	Mathematical Ideas
Use of graphical features of a spreadsheet package.	Use of symbolic notations to generate sequences. Symbolic and graphical representation of functions. Scale. Relationship between graphs of different gradients.

In this activity pupils are asked to plot a sequence generated by a linear function. They are then asked to generate sequences which when plotted produce parallel lines. Working in a spreadsheet environment has an advantage over using a graph-plotting package because pupils are able to compare the values in the spreadsheet table with the graph produced. In this respect the activity is very similar to the 'paper and pencil' activity of constructing a table and plotting a graph from this table of values.

	A	B	
1	x	y	
2	-5	-13	
3	-4	-10	
4	-3	-7	
5	-2	-4	
6	-1	-1	
7	0	2	
8	1	5	
9	2	8	
10	3	11	
11	4	14	
12	5	17	
13	6	20	
14	7	23	
15	8	26	

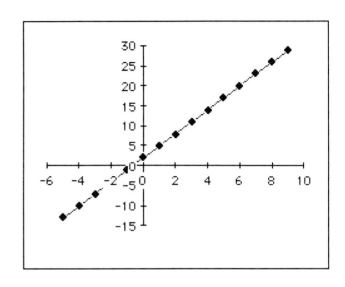

On your spreadsheet generate values for x.

In the next column generate values for y.

eg $y = 3x + 2$

Create a graph of the line

$y = 3x + 2$

In the next column of your spreadsheet, generate sequences using other functions of x.

Can you identify the set of functions that produce lines parallel to the line $y = 3x + 2$.

Investigate with different functions of x.

• The teacher has an important role both in supporting pupils to produce a graph in the spreadsheet environment, and in ensuring that they understand the graph produced. We found that it was important for pupils to have had previous 'paper and pencil' experience of graphing functions so that they understood how the line had been generated from x, y coordinates.

• After pupils have investigated the given function it is a good idea to let them investigate sequences generated by their own formulae.

• Teachers need to be aware that the scaling of the graphs may well be changed automatically when additional lines are plotted. They will need to discuss this with their pupils - particularly where polynomial sequences are investigated.

Investigating straight-line graphs: Richard and Abdul (two 12-year-olds) worked together on this task. Both pupils had been introduced to the graphing facilities available on their spreadsheet package. They had also previously used a spreadsheet to enter and copy relative rules. Richard and Abdul had no difficulty in setting up the spreadsheet and generating the sequence produced by the given function (y = 3x + 2). They were then shown how to produce a graphical representation of y against x (see Fig. 3.8).

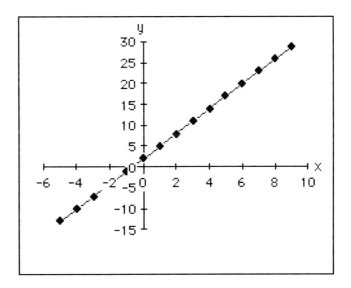

Fig 3.8: The graph of y = 3x + 2.

They attempted to add a second line to their graph. Initially they just experimented with plotting any additional sequences onto the graph, rather than attempting to produce a parallel line. When they were confident in handling the procedure to add a graphical representation of their sequence they returned to the problem in hand. Quite quickly they produced a line parallel to the y = 3x + 2 line. However, they had done this by defining a formula in column C which operated on the sequence in column B (=B2 + 7) rather than on the values of x in column A (see Fig. 3.9).

	A	B	C
1	x	y	z
2	-5	-13	=B2+7
3	-4	-10	
4	-3	-7	
5	-2	-4	
6	-1	-1	
7	0	2	
8	1	5	
9	2	8	
10	3	11	
11	4	14	
12	5	17	
13	6	20	

Fig 3.9: Generating a line parallel to y = 3x + 2: method 1.

The aim of the task was then re-explained. Richard immediately responded *'oh but that will be easy now'* and replaced the formula in column C with a the formula = (A2*3) + 9 (see Fig 3.10). He explained to his partner why this produced the same sequence as their previous formula.

	A	B	C
1	x	y	z
2	-5	-13	=(A3*3)+9
3	-4	-10	
4	-3	-7	
5	-2	-4	
6	-1	-1	
7	0	2	
8	1	5	
9	2	8	
10	3	11	
11	4	14	
12	5	17	
13	6	20	

Fig 3.10: Generating a line parallel to y = 3x + 2: method 2.

They then turned their attention to the graph. Because they had focused on the difference between the sequences (i.e. + 7) they very quickly noticed that the gap between the two parallel lines was also 7. Abdul suggested that they add a parallel line underneath their original. Richard realised that all they needed to do was to change the + 2 to either a smaller number or a negative number. Abdul suggested 0. When they plotted this line (y = 3x + 0), it passed through the origin. Richard pointed out that the last number in their formula (the constant) determined where the line crossed the y - axis and the gap between parallel lines, a deduction which had arisen from his exploration in the spreadsheet environment. The pair went on to plot two other graphs parallel to the original y = 3x + 2 before the session ended. In their next session the pair went on to look at the effect of changing the "3x" to other values. They discovered that this changed the slope of the line but the constant still determined where the line crossed the y - axis.

Sum, Average and Other Spreadsheet Functions

Most spreadsheet packages have a range of mathematical functions which can be used to simplify certain mathematical calculations. It is worth becoming aware of the functions available in your spreadsheet package because then you can decide when it is appropriate to introduce these functions to pupils. Ordering Clothes presented in Chapter 2 can be used to introduce pupils to the statistical function SUM which allows the sum of a column or row of cells to be calculated (see Fig. 2.16). Record Shop Prices and Guess the Inequality can be used to introduce pupils to the logical function IF. Examples of functions available in most packages include:

- Trigonometric functions e.g. SIN, COS, TAN, ATAN
- Arithmetic functions e.g. ABS, EXP, RAND
- Logical functions e.g. IF, TRUE, FALSE
- Statistical functions e.g. AVERAGE, SUM, STD.

Chapter 4 EXPRESSING AND EXPLORING MATHEMATICAL IDEAS

Introduction

This chapter presents a range of problems which involve pupils in expressing and exploring mathematical ideas. These problems are not necessarily more difficult than the introductory problems presented in Chapters 2 and 3, but they do assume that pupils are already confident in using a spreadsheet package. We are continually thinking of new problems which could be valuably solved within a spreadsheet environment and have included references to other useful sources of materials in the bibliography. We ourselves only started to generate new ideas for using spreadsheets after considerable experience of working with a spreadsheet package. We are confident that with the starting points provided in this chapter you and your pupils will begin to generate your own problems for using spreadsheets.

Algebraic Expressions

It is a widely reported research result that pupils have difficulty with the dynamic nature of the relationship between algebraic expressions. So, for example, when pupils are asked the question 'Which is bigger $2x$ or $2+x$?' they usually answer $2x$ because for them 'multiplication always makes bigger' and they do not usually consider the nature of the relationship as x varies. Maybe their incorrect responses reflect general misconceptions about the idea of a variable but it is more likely that pupils lack experience of this idea. The following activity aims to redress this balance.

Which is Bigger? (Activity 4.1)

In working on Activity 4.1 pupils are likely to use the following spreadsheet and mathematical ideas:

Spreadsheet ideas	Mathematical ideas
Naming a cell.	Variable.
Use of inequalities.	Interrelationship between two algebraic expressions.
Accuracy of the computer.	Equality/inequality of algebraic expressions.
	Continuous nature of decimal numbers.

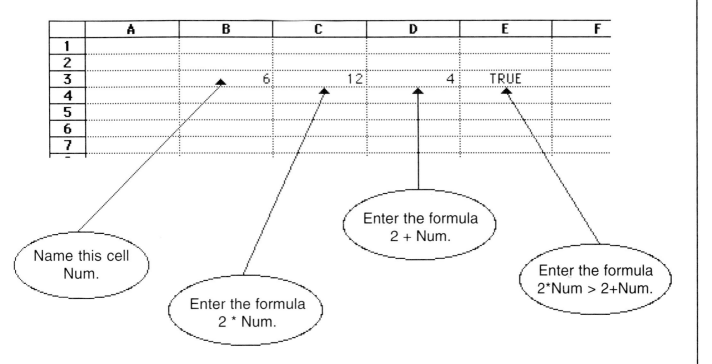

	A	B	C	D	E	F
1						
2						
3		6	12	4	TRUE	
4						
5						
6						
7						

Name this cell Num.

Enter the formula 2 * Num.

Enter the formula 2 + Num.

Enter the formula 2*Num > 2+Num.

Change the value in Num to investigate:

When is 2 + Num bigger than 2 * Num?

When is 2 * Num bigger than 2 + Num?

When are they the same?

Change the formulae to 3 * Num and 3 + Num

4 * Num and 4 + Num

• Within Activity 4.1 we have chosen to use the idea of naming a cell as a means of absolute reference because this presents pupils with a representation which is similar to the standard algebraic notation.

Understanding the dynamic nature of a variable. We have tried out Activity 4.1 with 12-year-old-pupils, Jo and Eleanor, who had previously had the experience of entering a formula with reference to a named cell (Activity 3.2). Jo and Eleanor were highly motivated when they worked on this rather abstract activity. We used their own names (i.e. JO and ELI) as variable names because this seemed to be a more accessible way of introducing them for the first time to the idea of a variable. Jo and Eleanor first of all wrote down single value answers to the questions posed on the activity sheet (e.g. as an answer to 'When is 2 + JO bigger than 2*JO' they wrote down 'When JO is 1'). The teacher nudged them into trying some more numbers which they proceeded to do using only positive whole numbers. Another nudge was needed to encourage them to use decimal and negative numbers. They finally became convinced that *'2 + JO is bigger than 2 * JO when JO is less than 2 and smaller when JO is more than 2'.*

They next changed the formulae to compare the expressions 3 + JO and 3 * JO, this time confidently using decimal numbers and recording their results on paper. Finally they explored the relationship between 4 + JO and 4 * JO. In solving this problem they discussed the relationship between 1/3 and 0.333333333. The computer could only present an approximation to 4/3, highlighting the restrictions of a computer environment.

• Collaboration, discussion and recording on paper are all important aspects of this activity. In talking together pupils are likely to use the spreadsheet formalism (e.g. *'4 plus JO is bigger than 4 times JO when JO is bigger than one and a third'*) to express their mathematical ideas.

• Another possible teacher intervention would be to suggest that the pupils replicate their formulae to use the spreadsheet to present their results (see Fig. 4.1). One advantage of some spreadsheet packages (e.g. EXCEL and MULTIPLAN) is that it is possible to name a column and so the more conventional-looking algebra formalism is preserved (Fig. 4.2 shows the formulae that generate the results shown in Fig. 4.1).

	A	B	C	D	
1					
2	-2	-4	0	FALSE	
3	-1.5	-3	0.5	FALSE	
4	-1	-2	1	FALSE	
5	-0.5	-1	1.5	FALSE	
6	0	0	2	FALSE	
7	0.5	1	2.5	FALSE	
8	1	2	3	FALSE	
9	1.5	3	3.5	FALSE	
10	2	4	4	FALSE	
11	2.5	5	4.5	TRUE	
12	3	6	5	TRUE	
13	3.5	7	5.5	TRUE	
14	4	8	6	TRUE	
15	4.5	9	6.5	TRUE	
16	5	10	7	TRUE	
17	5.5	11	7.5	TRUE	
18	6	12	8	TRUE	
19					

Fig. 4.1: Investigating inequalities (generated sequences).

	A	B	C	D	
1					
2	-2	=2*J0	=2+J0	=2*J0>2+J0	
3	-1.5	=2*J0	=2+J0	=2*J0>2+J0	
4	-1	=2*J0	=2+J0	=2*J0>2+J0	
5	-0.5	=2*J0	=2+J0	=2*J0>2+J0	
6	0	=2*J0	=2+J0	=2*J0>2+J0	
7	0.5	=2*J0	=2+J0	=2*J0>2+J0	
8	1	=2*J0	=2+J0	=2*J0>2+J0	
9	1.5	=2*J0	=2+J0	=2*J0>2+J0	
10	2	=2*J0	=2+J0	=2*J0>2+J0	
11	2.5	=2*J0	=2+J0	=2*J0>2+J0	
12	3	=2*J0	=2+J0	=2*J0>2+J0	
13	3.5	=2*J0	=2+J0	=2*J0>2+J0	
14	4	=2*J0	=2+J0	=2*J0>2+J0	
15	4.5	=2*J0	=2+J0	=2*J0>2+J0	
16	5	=2*J0	=2+J0	=2*J0>2+J0	
17	5.5	=2*J0	=2+J0	=2*J0>2+J0	
18	6	=2*J0	=2+J0	=2*J0>2+J0	

Fig. 4.2: Investigating inequalities (formulae).

Financial Modelling

Spreadsheets are a valuable tool for modelling 'real life' situations because they remove laborious calculations and allow pupils to explore the potential and implications of the model. In the business world spreadsheets are extensively used for financial modelling. For these problems we feel that it is more motivating for pupils to model a 'realistic' problem (e.g. to compare different savings schemes) starting by the collection of 'real' data. If it is not possible to collect more 'realistic' data we have found that <u>A Rich Aunt</u> is a good introductory problem. (This activity is card no. 1425 in the SMILE[1] mathematics scheme and it is shown in Fig. 4.3.) When solving this problem pupils are likely to use the following spreadsheet and mathematical ideas.

Spreadsheet ideas	Mathematical ideas
Replication of formulae containing relative references.	Modelling financial schemes.
Graphing.	Symbolic notation to express sequences.
	Exploration of behaviour of sequences and rates of growth.
	Summing of sequences.

• The formulae underlying the schemes suggested in this problem are reasonably straightforward for pupils to define. The spreadsheet can then be used to generate the yearly amount produced by each scheme. It does not, however, 'solve' the problem. Pupils need to examine the results of replicating their formulae carefully in order to make and justify their choice.

• Some pupils will generate the cumulative amounts they would receive for each scheme in order to make their decision, although in general we have found that they do not do this unless it is suggested to them.

Cumulating totals. Mikos and Sylvia, two lower-sixth form students (aged 16-17) who were re-taking mathematics GCSE, worked on this problem early on in their spreadsheet experience. They had previously experimented with entering and replicating formulae containing relative references, including defining formulae which contained more than one cell reference. Without much apparent difficulty, Mikos, under Sylvia's direction, entered the formulae to model the four schemes. They copied the formulae down into the next 30 cells (until the Aunt's age was 100) and saw that in the long run scheme D provided the greatest financial benefits.

At this point, although they had decided to generate the schemes until the Aunt reached 100 years, they made no other attempt to discuss her age and

[1]Secondary Mathematics Independent Learning Experience

You will need a calculator

A Rich Aunt

Bob has a rich aunt, who is a mathematician. She wrote this letter to Bob:

> Dove Cottage
> Brainage
> Hertfordshire
>
> Telephone 241
>
> Dear Bob
> Now that I am getting on, (I'm 70 today). I want to give you some of my money. I shall give you a sum each year, starting now. You can choose which of the following schemes you would like me to use.
>
> (a) £100 now, £90 next year, £80 the year after, and so on.
>
> (b) £10 now, £20 next year, £30 the year after, and so on.
>
> (c) £10 now, $1\frac{1}{2}$ times as much next year, $1\frac{1}{2}$ times as much again the year after that, and so on.
>
> (d) £1 now, £2 next year, £4 the year after, £8 the year after that, and so on.
>
> Of course, these schemes can only operate while I am alive. I look forward to hearing which scheme you choose, and why!
>
> Best wishes
>
> Aunt Lucy.

Reply to this letter.

Fig. 4.3: A rich aunt   (from SMILE 1425)

how this might affect their choice. A teacher intervention was made, suggesting that they sum the sequences to determine the cumulative amounts from each scheme. Sylvia was not sure how to do this on the spreadsheet and suggested that they needed to multiply the yearly amounts in schemes which involved multiplication. Mikos was not convinced, and seemed to realise that they needed to add the amount for the current year to the total for the preceding year, not having enough confidence either to explain this to his partner or to attempt to represent his idea on the spreadsheet. Eventually Sylvia started calculating the cumulative amounts on paper and this method seemed to provide her with the scaffolding she needed to enter an appropriate spreadsheet formula.

Having generated the cumulative amounts, they had a lengthy discussion about which scheme they would choose, taking into account the age of the Aunt. Sylvia still went for scheme D although she was aware that whether or not this turned out to be the most profitable depended on how long Aunt Lucy lived. Mikos was more tempted by scheme A. Although in the long run it ended up least profitable (*'do minus numbers mean we have to start paying her back?'*), it gave the largest immediate rewards.

• In spreadsheets with adequate graphing facilities, graphical representations of the schemes can also be explored.

Exploring graphical representations. Rachel and Rita, two second-year pupils (aged 12-13), had been exploring the graphing facilities available in EXCEL. They were given the <u>Rich Aunt</u> problem, and produced 3 graphs, showing the cumulative growth of the schemes over 5, 10 and 20 years (Figs. 4.4-4.6). Rachel and Rita used the graphical models of the scheme as a focus for discussing the relative advantages and disadvantages of each.

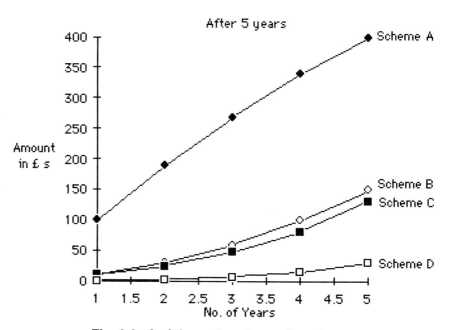

Fig 4.4: A rich aunt: return after 5 years

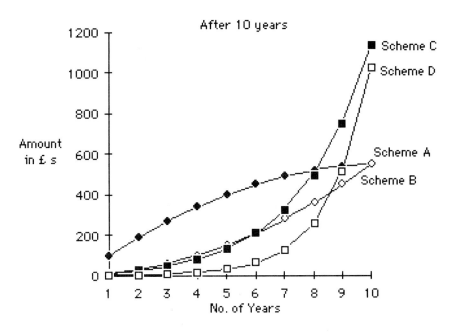

Fig 4.5: A rich aunt: return after 10 years

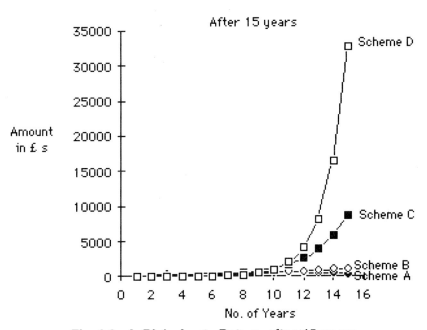

Fig 4.6: A Rich Aunt: Return after 15 years

Numerical Solutions of Equations

The facility to carry out and display a number of calculations at one time makes the spreadsheet a useful tool for solving problems using an iterative method: for example an iterative solution for finding square roots, the Newton Raphson method for solving equations or Simpson's rule for calculating integrals. Whereas it is possible to solve these types of problems in most computer programming languages, performing these calculations on a spreadsheet has the added advantage that the 'step by step' calculations can be displayed in a way which facilitates analysis of the iterative process. We present here two problems in this category and suggest that with experience pupils can choose to use a spreadsheet package to solve these types of problems as they occur within their normal mathematics curriculum. So for example if A-level pupils are learning about Simpson's rule for calculating integrals, we suggest that a spreadsheet package would make the process more accessible than performing the laborious calculations on a calculator.

Finding Square Roots (Activity 4.2)

The Finding Square Roots activity introduces pupils to a 'homing-in' iterative approach to finding square roots. Pupils can choose their own method for 'homing-in' on the square root but through exploration should learn the importance of being systematic in their search. In carrying out this activity pupils are likely to use the following spreadsheet and mathematical ideas:

Spreadsheet Ideas	Mathematical Ideas
Use of relative and absolute referencing.	Estimation.
Replicating a formula.	Trial and improvement methods.
Inserting blank rows in a spreadsheet.	Functions and variable.
Naming cells.	Decimal numbers.
	The continuous nature of the number line.
	The relationship between powers and roots.

• We have tried this task out with 12-13 year-old pupils. They were able to 'home-in' to the square root of 12 successfully. Some pupils preferred to lay out the successive approximations in columns extending across the spreadsheet and others were happy to program successive approximations into the same column.

• This activity helps pupils focus on the continuous nature of decimal numbers and gives them the opportunity to use an increasing number of decimal places.

• The final activity on the worksheet was chosen to give pupils a feel for why the square roots of 30 and 3 are not similar numbers, an idea which appears to be counter-intuitive.

FINDING SQUARE ROOTS

What is the square root of 12?

We generate the squares of numbers between 0 and 10.

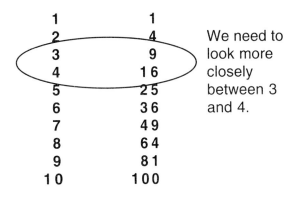

1	1
2	4
3	9
4	16
5	25
6	36
7	49
8	64
9	81
10	100

We need to look more closely between 3 and 4.

This time we start from 3 and use a difference of 0.1.

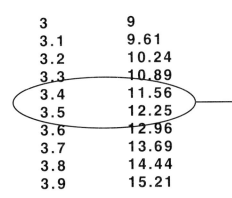

3	9
3.1	9.61
3.2	10.24
3.3	10.89
3.4	11.56
3.5	12.25
3.6	12.96
3.7	13.69
3.8	14.44
3.9	15.21

Now look more closely between 3.4 and 3.5.

Can you find a general method which allows you to change the START number and the DIFFERENCE number?

Use this to find:

$$\sqrt{30} \qquad \sqrt{3} \qquad \sqrt{0.3} \qquad \sqrt{0.03}$$

An Iterative Approach to Solving Cube Roots (Activity 4.3)

The following activity[2] is concerned with the iterative solution of equations which involves rearranging the equation in terms of x. So for example when solving the equation:

$$X^3 = 9$$

the equation is rearranged in terms of x and this rearrangement forms the basis of the iterative process:

For example:

$$0.5 \qquad X_{next} = \sqrt{\frac{9}{x}}$$

When carrying out this activity pupils are likely to use the following spreadsheet and mathematical ideas:

Spreadsheet ideas	Mathematical ideas
Use of relative and absolute referencing.	Iterative solution of equations.
Replication of formula using relative referencing.	Behaviours of iterative solutions e.g. converging, diverging, oscillating between roots.
Approximate nature of computer calculations.	Continuous nature of decimal numbers.

• When we worked with these ideas in the classroom we decided that pupils needed some previous experience of this approach to solving equations before using a spreadsheet package (for example Chapter 9 of Book Y5 SMP 11-16). Without this work away from the computer pupils found it difficult to understand how the 'iterative method' was related to the solution of an equation. With previous experience they realised that a spreadsheet provides a powerful tool for using this approach. We have chosen a problem in which three possible rearrangements of $x^3 = 9$ are provided and pupils are asked to investigate which of these will provide a solution. Spreadsheets can be used to show pupils the inefficiency of this 'rearranging' method before they are introduced to more efficient methods (for example Newton Raphson). This 'rearranging' approach can be

---

[2] This example has been influenced by the problem presented in chapter 9, Book Y5 of SMP 11-16.

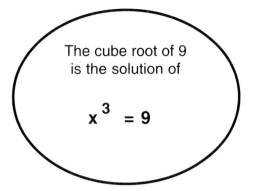

The cube root of 9
is the solution of

$$x^3 = 9$$

To iterate you need to rearrange this
equation in terms of x.
Possible rearrangements are:

$$x^3 = 9$$
$$x^2 = \frac{9}{x}$$
$$x = \sqrt{\frac{9}{x}}$$

$$x^3 = 9$$
$$x = \frac{9}{x^2}$$

$$x^3 = 9$$
$$x^4 = 9x$$
$$x^2 = \sqrt{9x}$$
$$x = (9x)^{\frac{1}{4}}$$

0.5

$$x_{next} = \sqrt{\frac{9}{x}}$$

0.5

$$x_{next} = \frac{9}{x^2}$$

0.5

$$x_{next} = (9x)^{\frac{1}{4}}$$

Use a spreadsheet to find out which of these
rearrangements will give the cube root of x.

Does it make any difference if you change the
starting value?

contrasted with the 'homing-in' method used in the <u>Finding Square Roots</u> activity.

• We tried out this activity with two 15-year-old pupils who were reasonably confident with mathematics and had started to work on this idea within Chapter 9 of Book Y5 SMP 11-16. The pupils were surprised that with some rearrangements they were able to find the root and with others they were not. They found that the initial value was a crucial factor influencing whether or not the iterative process converged. We encouraged the pupils to try negative numbers for the initial value.The activity can be extended to finding the cube root of any number including negative numbers.

• It is particularly important when carrying out these types of iterative calculations on a computer to consider the accuracy of the particular computer environment and how this might effect some of the decisions being made.

Two Ways of Expressing a Sequence (Activities 4.4 and 4.5)

The nature of a spreadsheet and the replicating process is closely related to mathematical sequences of numbers. We have already presented two activities in Chapter 3 (Activity 3.1 and Activity 3.2) related to this idea. We suspect that many pupils are confused between the two possible ways of generating both arithmetic and geometric sequences (i.e. using a universal rule or using a recurrence rule). Fig 4.7 shows a universal rule which generates an arithmetic sequence while Fig 4.8 shows the corresponding recurrence rule. Similarly, Fig 4.9 shows an example of a universal rule generating a geometric sequence and Fig 4.10 the corresponding recurrence rule. The recurrence rule is more often used in a spreadsheet environment but it is possible to use a spreadsheet to help convince pupils that both rules are valid and to help pupils understand the two methods. In working on Activities 4.4 and 4.5 the following mathematical and spreadsheet ideas will potentially be addressed:

Spreadsheet ideas	Mathematical ideas
Defining and replicating formulae containing both relative and absolute references.	Distinguishing between universal and recurrence formulae.
Naming cells.	Decimal and negative numbers.
Naming columns.	Importance of common difference as a link between the two representations.
	Symbolising general formulae for arithmetic and geometric sequences.

There are two ways of generating an arithmetic sequence:

POSITION IN SEQUENCE (n)	SEQUENCE
1	3
2	5
3	7
4	9
5	11
6	13
...	...

The **RECURRENCE** rule for this sequence is

1st term = 3
nth term = (n-1)th term + 2

The **UNIVERSAL** rule for this sequence

nth term = (n * 2) +1

Can you enter formulae to express both the RECURRENCE rules and the UNIVERSAL rules which generate the following arithmetic sequences?

POSITION IN SEQUENCE (n)	SEQUENCE 1	SEQUENCE 2	SEQUENCE 3	SEQUENCE 4
1	7	-3	9	3.1
2	10	-1	8	5.2
3	13	1	7	7.3
4	16	3	6	9.4
5	19	5	5	11.5
6	22	7	4	13.6
...	...	...	...	...

Can you enter a GENERAL Recurrence Rule that can generate all the sequences?

What about a GENERAL Universal Rule?

There are two ways of generating a geometric sequence:

POSITION IN SEQUENCE (n)	SEQUENCE
1	2
2	6
3	18
4	54
5	162
6	486
...	...

The **RECURRENCE** rule for this sequence is

1st term = 2
nth term = (n-1)th term * 3

The **UNIVERSAL** rule for this sequence is

nth term = 2 * 3$^{(n-1)}$

Can you enter formulae to express both the RECURRENCE rules and the UNIVERSAL rules which generate the following geometric sequences?

POSITION IN SEQUENCE (n)	SEQUENCE 1	SEQUENCE 2	SEQUENCE 3	SEQUENCE 4
1	1	-4	16	250
2	2	-12	-8	50
3	4	-36	4	10
4	8	-108	-2	2
5	16	-324	1	0.4
6	32	-972	-0.5	0.08
...	...	...	...	...

Can you enter a GENERAL Recurrence Rule that can generate all the sequences?

What about a GENERAL Universal Rule?

	A	B
1	x	f(x)
2		1 =3*A2+1
3		2
4		3
5		4
6		5
7		6
8		7
9		8
10		9
11		10
12		11
13		12

Fig. 4.7: Spreadsheet representation of Universal Rule:

$x_n = 3n + 1$

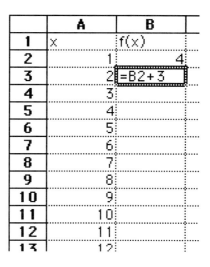

	A	B
1	x	f(x)
2		1	4
3		2 =B2+3
4		3
5		4
6		5
7		6
8		7
9		8
10		9
11		10
12		11
13		12

Fig. 4.8: Spreadsheet representation of of Recurrence Rule:

$x_n = x_{n-1} + 3; \; x_1 = 1$

	A	B
1	x	f(x)
2		1 =4*3^(A2-1)
3		2
4		3
5		4
6		5
7		6
8		7
9		8
10		9
11		10
12		11
13		12

Fig. 4.9: Spreadsheet representation of Universal Rule:

$x_n = 4 \cdot 3^{(n-1)}$

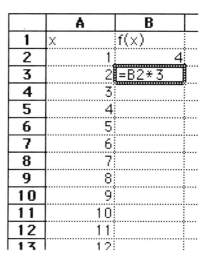

	A	B
1	x	f(x)
2		1	4
3		2 =B2*3
4		3
5		4
6		5
7		6
8		7
9		8
10		9
11		10
12		11
13		12

Fig. 4.10: Spreadsheet representation of Recurrence Rule:

$x_n = 3x_{n-1}; \; x_1 = 4$

Notes on Classroom use

• This activity explicitly encourages pupils to look for links between recurrence rules and universal rules. In our experience, both within computer and non-computer environments, pupils often find it easiest to spot the recurrence relationship by focusing on the common differences between consecutive terms in a sequence. Until our work with spreadsheets we had not observed pupils using this information as scaffolding to help uncover the universal rule. We have already described a situation in which two pupils did use this strategy in a previous activity (Activity 2.5 - see Chapter 2). We found that experience with Activities 4.4 and 4.5 also helps pupils see a link between the recurrence rule and the universal rule.

• In spreadsheet packages where pupils have the option of naming columns, they will be able to construct formulae closely resembling algebraic representations.

• If pupils are encouraged to name cells containing the first terms of the sequences and the common differences, then they will be able to define general formulae, for both recurrence rules and universal rules, which enable them to generate any arithmetic or any geometric sequence.

• An extension of these activities could involve the exploration of formulae which produce the sums of both arithmetic and geometric sequences. Pupils might be encouraged to look at the two ways in which the sums can be generated, again culminating in the production of general formulae, involving named cells, which can produce the sums for any arithmetic or any geometric sequence.

From recurrence to universal rules. Sonia and Julia, two third-year pupils (aged 13-14), had had experience of defining and replicating formulae, naming cells and columns of cells, and of graphing functions. They started work on Activity 4.5 by discussing the example given on the sheet. They noticed that the given sequence was the odd number sequence and found the recurrence rule *'obvious'*. Sonia was not sure about the universal rule - what it meant, how it was constructed or why it was included. She suggested to her partner that *'you only need to do the number before add 2'*. Julia then initiated a discussion in which she tried to explain why a universal rule was useful

Julia: *'You work this one out from here, the position, where it's called N, then you can do it for any one you like - the tenth odd number, the fiftieth and so on and on'*

Sonia: *'And on and on'*

Julia: *'Do you get it ?'*

Sonia: *'Ummm I think so'*

Julia: *'Let's do this one'*

When they attempted to generate 'Sequence 1' on the task sheet, they had no difficulty at all in entering the recurrence rule (see Fig 4.11). They then tried to determine the universal rule. Setting up the spreadsheet and entering the recurrence rule seemed to make the activity, and the distinction between the two rules, clearer to Sonia. She realised that for the universal rule it is not necessary to enter the first term of the sequence. The pair decided that they thought universal rules were probably 'better' than recurrence rules for this reason. It took them a long time to work out the universal rule underlying the sequence. Eventually they came up with a universal rule (see Fig 4.12). At this point Julia reflects on what they have done:

Julia: *'Hold on, hold on I think I 've found something, plus 3, times 3, plus 2 times 2, you times by your add on....does that work?'*

	A	B	C	
1				
2	pos (n)	S 1(r)	S 1 (u)	S 2
3	1	7		
4	2	=B3+3		
5	3			
6	4			
7	5			
8	6			
9	7			
10	8			
11	9			
12	10			
1 7	1 1			

Fig 4.11: Recurrence rule.

	A	B	C	
1				
2	pos (n)	S 1(r)	S 1 (u)	S 2
3	1	7	=A3*3+4	
4	2	10		
5	3	13		
6	4	16		
7	5	19		
8	6	22		
9	7	25		
10	8	28		
11	9	31		
12	10	34		
1 ⌐	1 1	⌐ ⌐		

Fig. 4.12 Universal rule.

They were then able to work out the rules underlying the remaining three sequences with relative ease.

After a teacher intervention, they named cells for both the common difference ('addon') and the first term ('firstn') of each sequence, attempting to enter formulae which would produce any arithmetic sequence. The recurrence rule formulae did not cause them too many difficulties, but they found the general universal rule more difficult. They knew they needed to multiply 'n' by the 'addon', but they thought that they then had to add the first term. The rules they produced are shown in Fig. 4.13 and the sequences produced in Fig. 4.14.

This cell is named **addon.**

This cell is named **firstn.**

	A	B	C	D
1	1.5			
2	4			
3		pos (n)	R	U
4		1	=firstn	=(B4*addon)+firstn
5		=B4+1	=C4+addon	=(B5*addon)+firstn
6		=B5+1	=C5+addon	=(B6*addon)+firstn
7		=B6+1	=C6+addon	=(B7*addon)+firstn
8		=B7+1	=C7+addon	=(B8*addon)+firstn
9		=B8+1	=C8+addon	=(B9*addon)+firstn
10		=B9+1	=C9+addon	=(B10*addon)+firstn
11		=B10+1	=C10+addon	=(B11*addon)+firstn
12		=B11+1	=C11+addon	=(B12*addon)+firstn
13		=B12+1	=C12+addon	=(B13*addon)+firstn
14		=B13+1	=C13+addon	=(B14*addon)+firstn

Fig 4.13 Sonia and Julia's general recurrence and universal rules (formulae).

	A	B	C	D
1	1.5			
2	4			
3		pos (n)	R	U
4		1	4	5.5
5		2	5.5	7
6		3	7	8.5
7		4	8.5	10
8		5	10	11.5
9		6	11.5	13
10		7	13	14.5
11		8	14.5	16
12		9	16	17.5
13		10	17.5	19
14		11	19	20.5

Fig 4.14 Sonia and Julia's general recurrence and universal rules (sequences).

They spent a little time attempting to debug this formula, however the lesson was nearing completion and they were not able to construct a general universal rule for themselves. In the end a possible representation was given to them by the teacher and the girls commented that they had been *'quite close really'*. Although they had identified a strategy to generate a universal rule from a recurrence rule for a specific arithmetic sequence, they could not at this point formalise this rule in a spreadsheet environment.

In the Limit (Activity 4.6)

Spreadsheets provide a good environment for investigating what happens to the terms of a sequence and the sum of a sequence as the number of terms increases. In the Limit is an activity which asks pupils to investigate the limiting process for the sum of a geometric sequence. Pupils do not need to know a rule for the sum of a geometric sequence in order to carry out this task because they can use a spreadsheet to calculate the sum cumulatively. In carrying out this activity pupils are likely to use the following spreadsheet and mathematical ideas:

Spreadsheet ideas	Mathematical ideas
Use of relative and absolute referencing.	Geometric sequences.
Replicating a formulae.	The sum of a geometric sequence.
Naming a cell.	Limits of sequences.

Drawing a graph of the numerical results of this investigation also provides another important representation of the limiting process (Fig. 4.15).

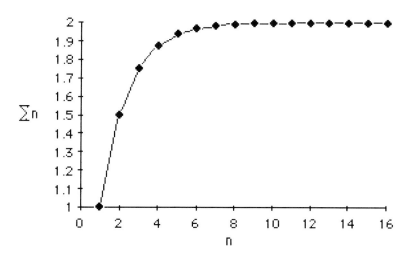

Fig. 4.15: Graphical representation of In the Limit.

Optimisation Problems

The spreadsheet environment makes it possible for students with no experience of calculus to investigate optimisation problems using iterative strategies. Problems like Maxbox (Fig. 4.16) are becoming popular spreadsheet activities (Wright, 1987).

Use a spreadsheet to generate the
geometric sequence

1, $\dfrac{1}{2}$, $\dfrac{1}{4}$, $\dfrac{1}{8}$, $\dfrac{1}{16}$ ....

and enter a formula to generate the sum
of this sequence.

	A	B	C	D	
1					
2		1	1		
3		0.5	1.5		
4		0.25	1.75		
5		0.125	1.875		
6		0.0625	1.9375		
7		---			

Enter the
sequence in this
column.

Calculate the sum of
the sequence in this
column.

What happens to the sum of the sequence as the
number of terms increases?

Investigate for the following sequences:

12, 6, 3, $1\dfrac{1}{2}$ .....

1, $\dfrac{1}{3}$, $\dfrac{1}{9}$, $\dfrac{1}{27}$ .....

54, -18, 6, -2 .....

Can you find any general rules?

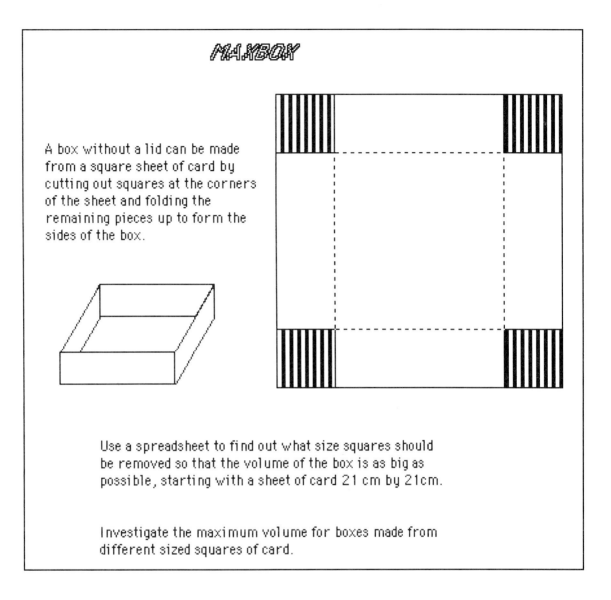

A box without a lid can be made
from a square sheet of card by
cutting out squares at the corners
of the sheet and folding the
remaining pieces up to form the
sides of the box.

Use a spreadsheet to find out what size squares should
be removed so that the volume of the box is as big as
possible, starting with a sheet of card 21 cm by 21cm.

Investigate the maximum volume for boxes made from
different sized squares of card.

Fig 4.16: MaxBox

We have found that this problem is a relatively difficult introductory
optimisation problem and present here a similar but more accessible
introductory activity (Maximum Areas, Activity 4.7).

Maximum Areas (Activity 4.7)

When pupils use Activity 4.7 they are likely to use the following
spreadsheet and mathematical ideas:

Spreadsheet Ideas	Mathematical Ideas
Entering and replicating a formula.	Continuous nature of decimal numbers. Trial and error methods. Formalising a generalisation. Use of brackets. Conjecturing.

• This type of problem is a good problem to introduce pupils to the algebraic idea of formalising a generalisation, because they will need to formalise a rule for working out the area of a rectangle given its perimeter before using the spreadsheet to calculate the maximum area.

Finding the maximum area. Jane and Alex started on this activity by negotiating a general rule:

Jane: *'Well first of all you want a rule for each one because if you know the length is one thing you can work out what the width is.......'*

Alex: *'So let's type the length in and then make a rule for the width from the length.......'*

The way in which the spreadsheet was set up on the activity sheet helped them to structure the problem.

Jane: *'Can we make a rule for the width and copy it down........'*

Alex: *'So......when you work out the width then the area equals that times that......and then you look down to see which is maximum.'*

Jane: *'Well I thought you could get....if you've got a total length of 15.....it says ....length is 1m......then you've got two lengths....is 2 metres...and so....and so you can have a rule of 15 minus 2 times the length divided by 2.......'*

They first of all entered the lengths (as given on the worksheet). They then negotiated the rule for the width as shown in Fig. 4.17, copied this down and finally entered a rule for the area (See Fig. 4.17) and copied this down.

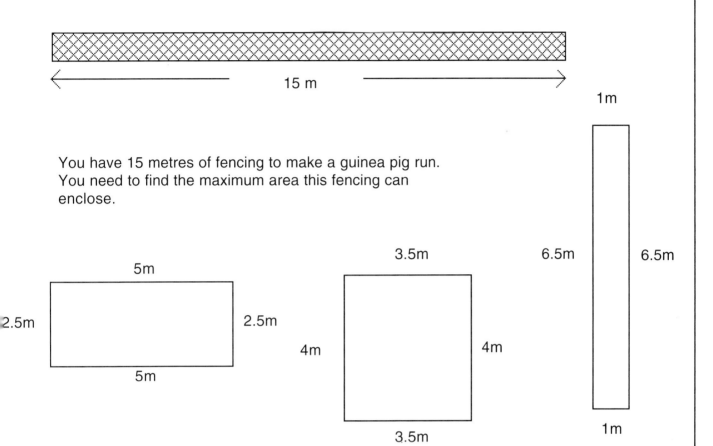

You have 15 metres of fencing to make a guinea pig run.
You need to find the maximum area this fencing can enclose.

	A	B	C	
1				
2				
3	LENGTH (m)	WIDTH (m)	AREA (m²)	
4	1			
5	1.5			
6	2			
7	2.5			
8	3			
9	3.5			
10	4			
11	4.5			
12	5			
13	5.5			
14	6			
15	6.5			
16	7			
17				

Use a spreadsheet to calculate the area for possible combinations of length and width.

Which combination would enclose the maximum area?

Work out the maximum areas you could enclose with the following total lengths of fencing:

15m
8m
22.5m

	A	B	C
1			
2			
3	LENGTH	WIDTH	AREA
4	1	=(15-(2*A4))/2	=A4*B4
5	1.5	=(15-(2*A5))/2	=A5*B5
6	2	=(15-(2*A6))/2	=A6*B6
7	2.5	=(15-(2*A7))/2	=A7*B7
8	3	=(15-(2*A8))/2	=A8*B8
9	3.5	=(15-(2*A9))/2	=A9*B9
10	4	=(15-(2*A10))/2	=A10*B10

Fig 4.17: Jane and Alex's spreadsheet for maximum area (length = 15).

There was considerable discussion about how many brackets they would need.

Alex: *'Should we just put all the brackets in to be safe....'*

From studying the table of values generated by the spreadsheet they were able to make a conjecture about the maximum area:

Jane: *'So it seems as if it's a maximum area when the lengths and width are the same'*

They then worked out that this would be when the length was 15/4 = 3.75 and recalculated the spreadsheet so that the length increased in intervals of 0.25. They then confirmed this rule by trying out the other given total lengths (8m, 22.5m)

Jane: *'Another way of checking would be to have it go up in 0.1 or something.....I think our theory is right.....'*

Jane and Alex then tried plotting the area against the length of the rectangle which produced a parabola (Fig. 4.18), adding another visual image to the idea of maximum.

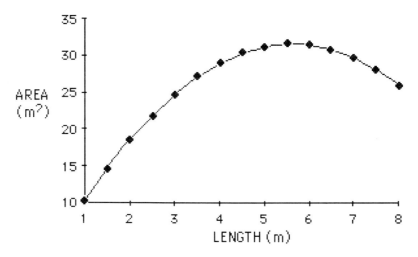

**Fig. 4.18: A graphical representation for maximum area.
(length = 22.5).**

Investigating Differences of Equations (Activity 4.8)

We have used this activity with both 12-13 year-old pupils and 16-17 year-old pupils and shall describe both sessions in detail, because they provide a good example of an investigation which would be suitable for an extended piece of mathematical work. It is also a particularly good task to convince sceptics of the power of a spreadsheet to recalculate large numbers of related cells when new values are entered. When carrying out this activity pupils are likely to use the following spreadsheet and mathematical ideas.

Spreadsheet Ideas	Mathematical Ideas
Entering and replicating formulae.	Quadratic and other polynomials.
Relative referencing.	General expression for a polynomial.
Naming a cell.	Differences of polynomials.
	Methods for working out a polynomial given the differences.
	Factorials.
	Differentiation.
	Conjecturing and proof.

Generate values for x in column A.

Enter and copy down a formula to represent a quadratic function in column B column (eg $x^2 + 3x + 1$).

In the third column, enter a formula which calculates the difference between consecutive terms in the sequence generated by the quadratic.

Copy this into adjoining columns until the difference becomes a constant.

	A	B	C	D
1				
2	1	5		
3	2	11	6	
4	3	19	8	2
5	4	29	10	2
6	5	41	12	2
7	6	55	14	2
8	7	71	16	2
9	8	89	18	2

For this quadratic the 2nd difference is always 2.

Change $x^2 + 3x + 1$ to $4x^2 + 3x + 1$

$$x^2 - 6x + 7$$
$$2x^2 + 5$$
$$3x^3 + 2x^2 + x - 1$$
$$2x^3 - 6x - 1$$
$$x^4$$

Can you predict what will happen?

The following equations have been lost. Can you work them out?

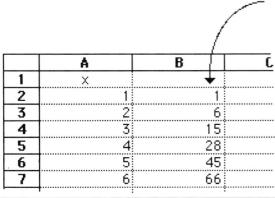

	A	B	C
1	x		
2	1	1	
3	2	6	
4	3	15	
5	4	28	
6	5	45	
7	6	66	

	A	B	C
1	x		
2	1	-3.5	
3	2	0	
4	3	9.5	
5	4	28	
6	5	58.5	
7	6	104	

• Four 12-13 year-old pupils working in pairs spent several sessions on this investigation. They all had previous spreadsheet experience, primarily involving defining and replicating formulae containing relative references.

Differences in polynomials. Daniel and Jack very quickly discovered that the second difference for quadratic functions is always a constant. It took them longer to determine the value of the constant as Jack suggested that they vary the coefficient of x^2 very early on in their investigation. Daniel noticed that the constant was always even and, after some discussion, was able to convince his partner to look at equations in which the coefficient of x^2 was always 1. After three attempts they were happy that the constant in this case would be 2, and as they varied the coefficient, could correctly predict the constant by multiplying the coefficient by 2.

They started looking at other polynomials. Daniel seemed to take control of directing the activity, Jack tended to copy the rules his partner entered and as the session went on made fewer predictions. They discovered very quickly that *'you can say the number of steps from the highest power'*. This led Daniel to suggest they look at x^3, x^4, x^5 and so on.

By the time they got to x^5, Daniel was busy scribbling down on scraps of paper. Before they generated the fifth difference, Daniel communicated his idea to Jack, which was that the constant would be 120. Jack thought that this was rather unlikely as 120 seemed much larger than the constants they had previously obtained. Jack summoned the teacher and Daniel re-explained his idea of 120. Jack then entered and copied the rule which generated the fifth difference. They jumped up in excitement when it did indeed generate a constant of 120. It was suggested to the pair that they try altering the coefficient of x^5. Daniel said they didn't need to – he already knew what would happen, he 'proved' this by entering the polynomial $3x^5 + 2x^4 + x + 9$, for which he correctly predicted a fifth difference of 360.

This pair next went on to the problem of uncovering the polynomial expressions behind given sequences of differences. They adopted a strategy whereby they entered the numbers in the given sequence and worked out how many columns of differences before a constant was generated. This enabled them to determine both the highest power of x in the expression and its coefficient. Daniel then worked out the rest of the expression basically through trial and error. This strategy was successful only when the sequences were generated by quadratic expressions.

Keeping records. John and Roger decided that they would record all their findings on the spreadsheet as they went along. Figs 4.19 and 4.20 show two parts of the spreadsheet they were working on.

	A	B	C	D	E	
1	X=???	Function	Step=3			Fun
2	1	3	Constant=6			
3	2	12	9			
4	3	33	21	12		
5	4	72	39	18	6	
6	5	135	63	24	6	
7	6	228	93	30	6	
8	7	357	129	36	6	
9	8	528	171	42	6	
10	9	747	219	48	6	
11	10	1020	273	54	6	
12	11	1353	333	60	6	
13	12	1752	399	66	6	
14	13	2223	471	72	6	
15	14	2772	549	78	6	
16	15	3405	633	84	6	

Fig. 4.19: Keeping a record.

	R	S	T	U	Y	
1	Function	Step=4				Fur
2	6	Constant=24				
3	21	15				
4	86	65	50			
5	261	175	110	60		
6	630	369	194	84	24	
7	1301	671	302	108	24	
8	2406	1105	434	132	24	
9	4101	1695	590	156	24	
10	6566	2465	770	180	24	
11	10005	3439	974	204	24	
12	14646	4641	1202	228	24	
13	20741	6095	1454	252	24	
14	28566	7825	1730	276	24	
15	38421	9855	2030	300	24	

Fig. 4.20: Keeping a record.

John and Roger spent 2 mathematics lessons, (approximately two and a half hours) constructing this spreadsheet. At the end of this time they were able to make accurate predictions for any polynomial. They had discovered that the number of steps it took before the difference became constant corresponded to the highest power of x in the expression and that the constant was the factorial of this number multiplied by the coefficient of the highest power of x.

Factorials and differentiation. The activity was also carried out with a class of twelve 16-17 year-olds who were studying A-level mathematics and were already familiar with entering and replicating formulae. We decided to organise this as a group activity so that the pupils were encouraged to discuss their mathematical conjectures and knew that they had some responsibility to share their ideas with the whole class at the end of the session. At the beginning of the session they were divided into three groups, each group being given a handout (Fig. 4.21) explaining the group activity and a copy of the activity sheet (Activity 4.8).

DIFFERENCES OF EQUATIONS: GROUP ACTIVITY

We have divided you into groups of four. We would like you to work on Investigating Differences of Equations in a group. By the end of the session we want you to report back your group's findings to the rest of the class.

Within your group you should:

- decide on a strategy for working effectively as a group,

- choose someone who will report back to the rest of the class at the end of the session,

- allow time to discuss as a group before reporting back,

- when you finally come up with some hypotheses think about how you can justify them mathematically.

Fig. 4.21: Organising a group activity.

The pupils chose to work at the computer in groups of four although there were enough computers available for them to work in pairs. We describe here in detail the work of one of these groups: Helen, Martin, Jim and Paula. They started the activity by programming the spreadsheet to calculate the differences for the specified quadratic ($x^2 + 3x + 1$) using the spreadsheet package VIEWSHEET. Martin typed and the other three chorused the instructions for programming the spreadsheet. They calculated the differences for two further quadratics and came up with a conjecture:

'It is the 2nd difference for x squared ..it could be the 3rd difference for x cubed and the 4th difference for x to the fourth ...'

They were able to predict correctly that the constant would be 4 for the quadratic $2x^2 + 5$, before trying this out at the computer.

They then predicted that for a cubic there would be a common difference of 3 at the third difference. When the result of 6 appeared this caused more discussion and exploration.

'Oh hang on this has got an x squared in it as well hasn't it...'

'Let's try "3x cubed plus 3x squared" and see what happens....'

'We'd better do the ones on the sheet...'.

'Why don't we just try 3x cubed ....'

After more exploration they wrote down the following.

$x^2 + 3x + 1$ 2nd difference   is always 2.

$4x^2 + 3x + 1$ ''   ''   8

$x^2 - 6x + 7$ ''   ''   2

we predicted, correctly, that the no. infront of the x^2 is multiplied by 2 to give the 2nd common difference.

$2x^2 + 5$ 2nd difference is always 4.

x^3 3rd differce is always 6.

$3x^2$ ~~xxxxxxxxxx~~   ''   ''   18.

$3x^3 + 2x^2 + x - 1$ ''   ''   18 .)

We thought the x^2 factor may have an influence on the common difference but it appears it is only the first term that sets the common difference

$2x^3 - 6x - 1$ 3rd difference always 12.

x^4 4th '' '' 24.

The product of the powers up to + including the ~~tree~~ term with the highest power.

eg. x^4 — $4 + 3 + 2 \times 1 = 24$ ✓.

The power of the highest term gives the column in which a constant difference occurs.

General formula :- common difference = (highest power)!

Fig. 4.22:   **Conjectures generated by differences of equations activity.**

Helen said *'If you want to put it succinctly you can say it's the highest power factorial.'*

By now they were sure about their conjectures and they worked on predicting equations from the first differences.

In order to work out the 'lost equations' they used the spreadsheet to calculate the common differences and then used a mixture of deduction and trial and error to work out the 'lost equations' (see Fig. 4.23). They were then able to use the spreadsheet to check out their conjectures.

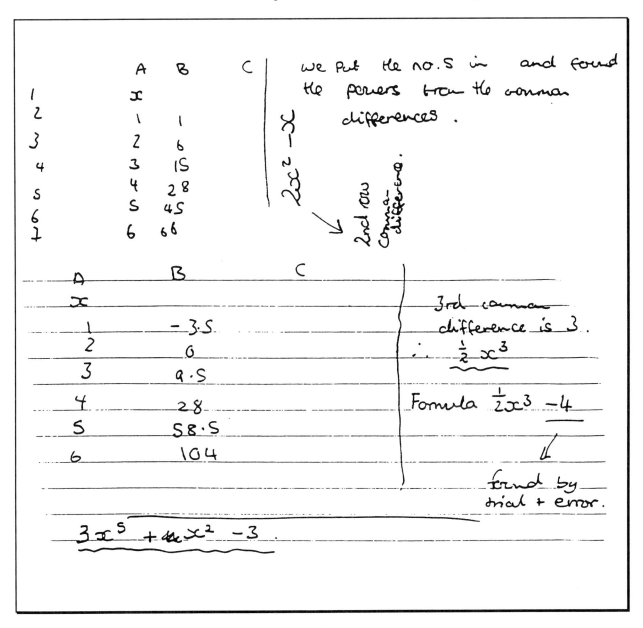

Fig. 4.23: Finding the 'lost' equations.

Finally these four pupils extended the task by dividing into groups of two and constructing the first differences of a polynomial to present to the other pair. When they all came together at the end of the lesson they were able to discuss their results with the whole class and the following issues arose.

- Some pupils had devised a rule in terms of factorial and others in terms of the derivative. The class discussed the equivalence of these two rules.

- The class discussed a more efficient way of calculating the 'lost' equation, given the first difference, to avoid the trial and error methods they had used.

- The pupils discussed what would constitute a mathematical proof of their conjectures and decided that they would work on this for their homework. We believe that this type of computer activity could provide an important basis for mathematical proof. Pupils become convinced of their rules, an important step before investing the necessary energy in constructing a mathematical proof.

Strange Behaviour and Chaos (Activity 4.9)

One area of mathematics which is heavily dependent on computers is the study of chaotic behaviour in seemingly ordered and determined feedback systems of the form $x_{n+1} = f(x_n)$. Totally predictable equations can produce unpredictable behaviour – equations which are being used to model ideas within natural systems. Activity 4.9, <u>Strange Behaviour and Chaos,</u> involves exploring the behaviour of the mapping $x_{n+1} = Ax_n (1 - x_n)$ which can be used to model population growth.

> ' By the 1950s several ecologists were looking at variations of that particular equation, known as the logistic difference equation. In Australia, for example, W. E. Ricker applied it to real fisheries. Ecologists understood that the growth-rate parameter (ie the parameter A) represented an important feature of the model. In the physical systems from which these equations were borrowed, that parameter corresponded to the amount of heating, or the amount of non-linearity. In a pond it might correspond to the fecundity of the fish, the propensity of the population not just to boom but also to bust ('biotic potential' was the dignified term). The question was, how did these differential parameters affect the ultimate destiny of a changing population?' (Gleick, 1988, p63).

Changing this parameter A is the focus of the <u>Strange Behaviour and Chaos</u> investigation in which pupils are likely to use the following spreadsheet and mathematical ideas.

Spreadsheet Ideas	Mathematical Ideas
Defining and replicating formulae containing both relative and absolute references. Naming cells.	Iterative solution of equations. Accuracy of computational methods. Convergence and divergence. Period doubling. Chaotic behaviour.

STRANGE BEHAVIOUR AND CHAOS

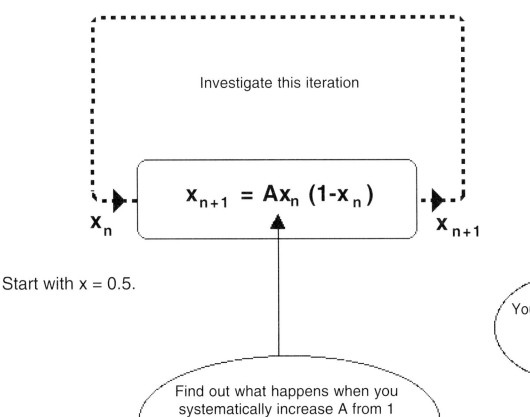

Investigate this iteration

$$x_{n+1} = Ax_n(1-x_n)$$

x_n x_{n+1}

Start with x = 0.5.

You will need at least 300 iterations.

Find out what happens when you systematically increase A from 1 to 4.
Keep the starting value the same.

Graphs make it easier to see what happens.

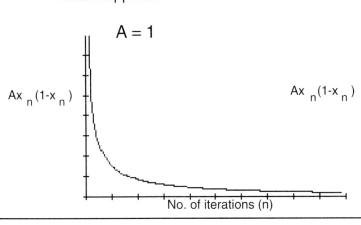

A = 1

$Ax_n(1-x_n)$

No. of iterations (n)

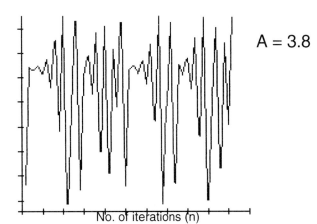

A = 3.8

$Ax_n(1-x_n)$

No. of iterations (n)

• We have tried this activity out with several 16-18 year-old pupils and have also used it with mathematics teachers attending in-service courses. It is important to have some understanding of both iterative processes and how to use a spreadsheet to represent iterative processes before carrying out this activity.

• By increasing the value of the parameter A pupils can observe how the behaviour of the iteration changes. Initially it is in a steady state and the iterative process converges to one root. As the value of A changes and becomes greater than 3 the period doubles and the process converges to two roots. This period doubling (bifurcation process) continues until eventually the period has doubled infinitely often and a chaotic state is reached. This process can be represented by plotting graphs of the iterated values against the number of iterations after first iterating a few hundred times (see Figs. 4.25 and 4.26).

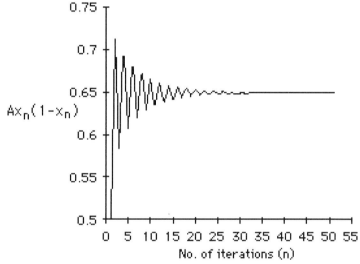

Fig. 4.25: Values of $x_{n+1} = 2.85x_n (1 - x_n)$

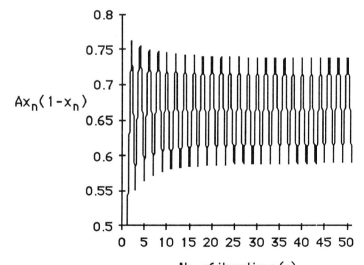

No. of iterations (n)
Fig. 4.26: Values of $x_{n + 1} = 3.1x_n (1 - x_n)$

It is possible to plot a graph which represents all the behaviour of the iterative process in one diagram (Fig. 4.27) and although this could be done in a spreadsheet environment we suggest that it could alternatively become the focus of a class activity. As pupils discover new behaviours for different values of A they can plot these on a collective 'graph'. This activity then encourages them to focus more precisely on the behaviour of the iteration process for different values of A and discourages unreflective 'whizzy effects' activity.

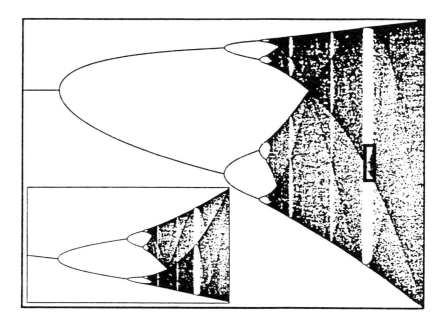

**Fig. 4.27: The Fig-Tree from Devlin, K (1988)
Mathematics: The New Golden Age.**

Ian Stewart (1985) has called this the fig-tree in honour of Feigenbaum, an American physicist who discovered that there is a constant ratio between successive values of the bifurcation process (the Feigenbaum ratio). Pupils could investigate the value of this ratio. Similar patterns are also produced with other mappings (for example $x_{n+1} = k \, \mathrm{Sin}(x_n)$) and this is another possible extension to the investigation.

Chapter 5 DIFFERENCES BETWEEN SPREADSHEET PACKAGES

Introduction

In the preceding chapters we have presented a range of activities in which the spreadsheet can be used as a tool to support and encourage pupils to explore and express mathematical ideas. We have presented a number of activities which exploit features offered in varying degrees by the spreadsheet packages available in schools. The packages which we have worked with include:

- GRASSHOPPER (BBC, Nimbus),
- VIEWSHEET (BBC),
- LOGISTIX (Archimedes, Nimbus),
- MULTIPLAN (Nimbus, Macintosh),
- EXCEL (Nimbus, Macintosh).

In this chapter the differences between these packages are described in terms of both the ease of use and the availability of different features. Throughout the book we have chosen to use the EXCEL representation of formulae, etc. In this chapter we describe how teachers may want to alter some of the activity sheets slightly so that they more closely resemble the representations used in the package available in their own school.

The features we describe are:

- cell reference style,
- entering data,
- entering and replicating formulae,
- editing formulae,
- absolute references and naming cells,
- functions,
- graphing,
- databases and tables,
- macros.

Cell Reference Style

As previously described, a spreadsheet is like a big electronic table, made up of a number of cells arranged in rows and columns. The labelling of the rows and columns varies according to the spreadsheet package. This labelling convention determines the way in which cells are referenced. We have come across two distinct cell reference styles: most spreadsheet packages use the 'A1' style of referencing cells (shown in Fig. 5.1). Of the spreadsheets we have worked with, GRASSHOPPER, VIEWSHEET, LOGISTIX and EXCEL all use this cell reference style.

	A	B	C	D	
1					
2					
3					
4					
5					
6					
7					
8					
9					
10					

Fig 5.1: 'A1' style of cell referencing.

A different cell reference style, 'R1C1' is used in the MULTIPLAN spreadsheet package (and also an available option in the EXCEL package). Fig. 5.2 shows this convention.

	1	2	3	4	5
1					
2					
3					
4					
5					
6					
7					
8					
9					
10					

Fig 5.2: 'R1C1' style of cell referencing.

We have used the 'A1' convention throughout this book, both in our illustrations of pupils' work and on the activity sheets. Teachers working with the MULTIPLAN package may find it useful to modify some of the earlier activity sheets to reflect the 'R1C1' style - we have found however that most pupils and teachers with whom we worked were able to use the 'A1' activity sheets without alterations being necessary.

Throughout this book whenever we illustrate a spreadsheet, the gridlines between the cells have always been displayed. We think this makes it easier to keep track of exactly where you are on the sheet. In some of the spreadsheet packages used in schools the gridlines are not displayed (see for example Fig 5.3)

The size (in terms of the number of rows and columns) of a spreadsheet also varies from package to package. In general, we have found it useful to work with very large spreadsheets (LOGISTIX has 2048 rows and 1024 columns and EXCEL has 16384 rows and 256 columns). This is especially important when working on activities such as investigating the behaviour of iterations (for example Activity 4.9). However, for the majority of our activities the size of the spreadsheet is not likely to be a problem.

```
 A   SLOT=A1
CONTENTS=*Blank*


0              . . . . . . .A. . . . . . .B. . . . . . .C. . . . . .
 . . . . . .1>
 . . . . . .2
 . . . . . .3
 . . . . . .4
 . . . . . .5
 . . . . . .6
 . . . . . .7
 . . . . . .8
 . . . . . .9
 . . . . .10
 . . . . .11
 . . . . .12
 . . . . .13
 . . . . .14
 . . . . .15
 . . . . .16
 . . . . .17
 . . . . .18
 . . . . .19
```

Fig. 5.3: VIEWSHEET.

Another important distinction between spreadsheet packages is whether or not they are 'mouse-driven'. In 'mouse-driven' spreadsheets (for example EXCEL and the Macintosh version of MULTIPLAN) the cells are accessed by clicking on them with the mouse. In the other packages cell are accessed by using arrow keys to move the cursor.

Entering Data

In all spreadsheet packages it is possible to enter text and numbers into any of the cells on the spreadsheet package. It is important that entering data should be as straightforward as possible. A problem we have encountered when working with some spreadsheet packages, is that the procedure for entering text is different from the procedure for entering numbers. In both GRASSHOPPER and MULTIPLAN (Nimbus), we have observed occasions when this has resulted in numbers being accidently entered as text. Subsequent attempts to use this data in formulae are greeted by an error message and for those in the early stages of spreadsheet use this is particularly confusing and frustrates their attempts to make sense of the way formulae are constructed. Teachers working with these packages need to be aware of how to help their pupils debug this problem. In other packages, the spreadsheet is able to determine for itself whether the data entered into a particular cell should be treated as text or numbers.

Entering and Replicating Formulae

In general, the representation of a formula depends on the cell reference style of the spreadsheet package. In packages adhering to the 'A1' style, the address of the referenced cell appears in the formula. In spreadsheets using the 'R1C1' style, formulae are symbolised relatively, that is the referenced cell is represented in terms of its relationship to the cell containing the formula. Figs 5.4 and 5.5 show how the same formula would be represented according to these different styles.

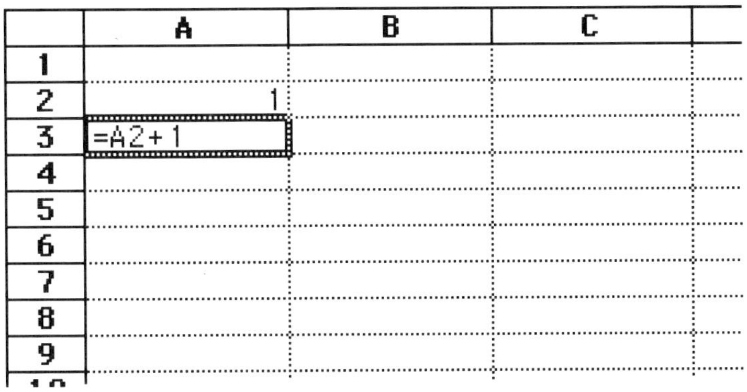

Fig. 5.4: 'A1' formula representation.

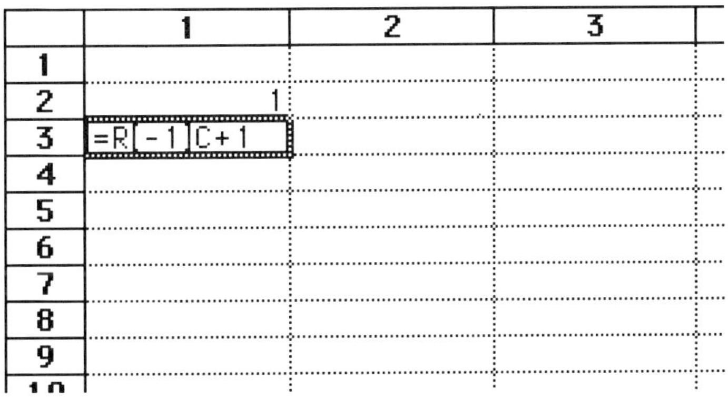

Fig. 5.5: 'R1C1' formula representation.

As we have used the 'A1' style throughout this book, the illustrated formulae do not correspond to the formulae produced by the MULTIPLAN package. We include in this chapter an alternative version of Activity 2.1, Guess the Formula, to illustrate the kinds of changes teachers working with 'R1C1' type spreadsheets may consider making.

There are some superficial differences between the formulae representations of the spreadsheet packages which use the 'A1' style. In all our examples formulae are preceded by an '=' sign as is the convention in EXCEL. For users of VIEWSHEET and GRASSHOPPER no sign is used to signify a formula and the LOGISTIX convention is to use a '+' sign to signify a formula[1]. Teachers may consider making these slight alterations to some of the activity sheets.

---

[1] In fact this itself has proved to be a potential source of confusion for those beginning their spreadsheet experience, when they are not sure when '+' sign represents the start of a formula definition and when it represents the addition operation.

	1	2	3
1			
2			
3		6	
4			
5			
6			
7			

Without letting your partner see what you are doing, enter a number into a cell.

In another cell enter a formula which does something to this number.

	1	2	3
1			
2			
3			6
4			=R[-1]C[-1]
5			
6			
7			

This formula takes the number from the cell in one row above and one column before and adds 3 to it.

Your partner must try to work out your formula.

	1	2	3
1			
2			
3		6	
4			9
5			
6			
7			

Your partner can only change this number.

Check the idea by entering it as a formula and comparing the results.

The representation of a replicated formula also varies depending on the cell referencing style. In GRASSHOPPER, VIEWSHEET, LOGISTIX and EXCEL ('A1' style), when a formula containing a relative reference is copied the formulae automatically change so that the referenced cell always maintains the same physical relationship to the cell containing the formula (Fig 5.6). In MULTIPLAN ('R1C1' style), a formula containing a relative reference does not change when it is copied, the symbolisation of the formula already represents the physical relationship between the referenced cell and the cell containing the formula (Fig 5.7).

	A	B	C	
1				
2	1			
3	=A2+1			
4	=A3+1			
5	=A4+1			
6	=A5+1			
7	=A6+1			
8	=A7+1			
9	=A8+1			

Fig. 5.6: A1 representation of a replicated formula.

	1	2	3	
1				
2	1			
3	=R[−1]C+1			
4	=R[−1]C+1			
5	=R[−1]C+1			
6	=R[−1]C+1			
7	=R[−1]C+1			
8	=R[−1]C+1			
9	=R[−1]C+1			

Fig. 5.7: R1C1 representation of a replicated formula.

In terms of supporting pupils' use of spreadsheets, each style carries with it possible advantages and disadvantages. For spreadsheets using the 'A1' style the generality of a formula is not expressed in the syntax. Initially it may be that the automatic changing of the formula will undermine learners' feelings of control over their work. On the other hand, we are concerned with the use of spreadsheets to support mathematics learning and, in spreadsheets using the 'A1' style, the spreadsheet formula is more accessible and resembles more closely algebraic rules. This should make it easier for learners to make links between spreadsheet formalisations and algebra symbolism. From our observations of pupils and teachers working with different packages, learners seem more readily able to reflect on the 'A1+1' type formula, than the 'R[-1]C+1' type, particularly in the early stages of spreadsheet use. Additionally, it does not seem to be too difficult for learners to reflect on the way the formula has changed in the process of replication, provided that this is introduced at an appropriate point in the spreadsheet experience.

Given the importance of the use of formulae in terms of mathematics learning, and our observation that defining and understanding formulae appear to be the most significant obstacles for pupils to negotiate in order to use the spreadsheet effectively, it is also important to consider the relative ease with which formulae can be entered across the different packages.

In the GRASSHOPPER package, defining even a fairly simple formula requires a relatively lengthy series of moves (involving both space bar and the return key). It is easy for pupils to lose track of their initial intentions and become bogged down in this process. Also in this package, the cell containing the formula is not specified until after the formula is constructed. Because of the importance of the physical relationships between cells, this can result in pupils becoming frustrated if they inadvertently enter a formula into the 'wrong' cell. Although the actual process of entering formulae is not too complicated in VIEWSHEET, we have found that, in general, both pupils and teachers need to refer more frequently to manuals or step-by-step guides when using this package – it seems less easy to explore the available possibilities. In all the remaining packages, EXCEL, LOGISTIX and MULTIPLAN, the actual process of entering formulae is relatively easy to get to grips with. We prefer the 'mouse-driven' packages to those in which the cursor is controlled by the arrows keys, because it is generally easier to keep track of the cell into which the formula is entered in 'mouse-driven' packages.

Editing Formulae

As with any computer-based activity, debugging is a potentially important problem-solving strategy. In a spreadsheet environment the most crucial aspect of debugging is dealing with formulae which produce unexpected results. To encourage pupils to reflect on processes for themselves, they need to be able to edit already defined formulae easily. This not only allows learners to reflect on the meaning of their formulae, it also gives them an opportunity to investigate formulae by changing one aspect and comparing the results. Editing formulae is fairly straightforward in both EXCEL and LOGISTIX. In GRASSHOPPER, pupils are not able to edit previously defined formulae. It is possible to edit formulae in MULTIPLAN and VIEWSHEET, but this involves remembering rather meaningless combinations of control keys, etc. So in GRASSHOPPER, MULTIPLAN and VIEWSHEET, pupils start again with a new formula definition rather than editing their already defined formula.

Absolute References and Naming Cells

In the preceding section on replicating formulae, the focus was formulae containing relative references, in which the physical relationship between the cell containing the formula and the referenced cells is always preserved. In exploring some of the mathematical activities in this book, it is necessary to refer to a particular cell in a formula without wanting this cell to change in a relative way when the rule is copied (an absolute reference). For example, you might want to generate a general rule for an arithmetic sequence where the difference between terms is specified in a particular cell on your spreadsheet (see Activity 3.1). All spreadsheets allow the possibility for defining rules containing absolute references, but the accessibility of this facility varies according to the different packages. In GRASSHOPPER, absolute references are made by the pressing of a particular key in the process of formula definition. In VIEWSHEET, in contrast to all the other packages, references are not automatically assumed to be relative and users are asked to specify each time they reference a cell whether they want this reference to 'change' (relative) or not (absolute).

In EXCEL, LOGISTIX and MULTIPLAN there are two ways of making absolute references. One way involves changing the notation used for a formula, and the other way involves naming a cell. We have found that most people find it easier to understand the process of absolute references by naming cells. After a cell has been given a name, then whenever this name is used in a formula it will always refer to the contents of the named cell. The possibility of naming rows or columns is also a useful facility. This means that, in both MULTIPLAN and EXCEL, naming can be used to define general formulae which correspond even more closely to algebraic representations, helping learners to make links across these two environments. In the LOGISTIX package it is also possible to name ranges of cells, although accessing cells within, say, a named column, seems rather problematic.

The EXCEL package also offers the potential to define a formula containing a reference which is partly absolute and partly relative (a mixed reference) so, for example, cells are accessed relatively across columns but the same row is always referred to.

Functions

All the spreadsheet packages offer functions which can be used within the definition of formulae. GRASSHOPPER was designed for use with primary age pupils and so only offers a restricted range of functions. The other packages all offer a large variety of functions, including arithmetic, trigonometric, statistical and logical functions (in general, the more powerful the software, the more functions are offered).

Graphing

Some of the activities included in this book have involved graphing the functions produced by spreadsheet formulae. In general, the graphing facilities available on all the currently available packages are either rather complicated to use or somewhat limited in what they offer. The MULTIPLAN spreadsheet itself does not have graphing facilities, but data from the spreadsheet can be used within separate graphing packages (e.g. MULTIGRAPH), others have a graphing option that can be viewed separately from the spreadsheet (e.g. GRASSHOPPER and LOGISTIX). When using MULTIPLAN, GRASSHOPPER and LOGISTIX it is not possible to view the numeric data and the graphical data simultaneously. In VIEWSHEET, it is possible to produce bar charts. However they are particularly inaccessible and relatively limited in their application. In EXCEL, graphs can be viewed at the same time as spreadsheets so that two representations of the same function can be seen simultaneously. Also extra functions can be added to the same graph (when investigating common properties of parallel lines, for example). Fig 5.8 illustrates the numeric and graphical representations resulting from iterating a function, making it easier to describe and investigate the behaviour of this iteration.

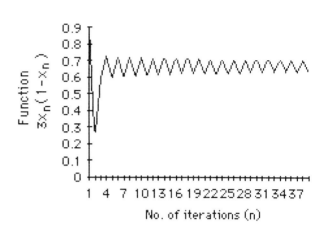

	A	B	
1		3ᵌx*(1-x)	
2		0.9	
3		0.27	
4		0.5913	
5		0.72499293	
6		0.59813454	
7		0.72110883	
8		0.60333265	
9		0.71796709	
10		0.60747104	
11		0.71534992	
12		0.61087323	
13		0.71312138	
14		0.61373783	
1E		0.71110113	

Fig. 5.8: Simultaneous numeric and graphical representation of the iteration $x_{n+1} = 3x_n(1-x_n)$.

Databases and Tables

Both EXCEL and LOGISTIX offer the facility to set up part of a spreadsheet as a database. So, for example, pupils working on a class project involving data handling would be able to record and interrogate data on the spreadsheet, and make use of the available statistical functions.

A further feature available in the EXCEL package is the use of one input or two input tables, which can be used to tabulate automatically a range of inputs to a particular formula. One possible use in mathematics might be to explore the results of various inputs to a formula containing two variables. Fig 5.9 shows how a table produces the results of the function $4x+3y$ for a range of values for x and y so, for example, it is possible to see two different solutions for $4x+3y = 26$ ($x = 5$, $y = 2$ and $x = 2$, $y = 6$) at a glance.

Macros

Another potentially useful feature available within the EXCEL package is the use of macros. There are two different kinds of macros that can be defined in this package: 'function macros', which can be used to create further functions to be added to those already available, and 'record macros', which record any sequence of actions which can subsequently be replayed.

Record macros have two possible uses in terms of mathematics learning: a macro could be set up to deal with complicated sequences such as when graphing data, or macros could be used to record pupils' progress within an activity, giving insight into the strategies they adopt as well as the formalisations they finally construct.

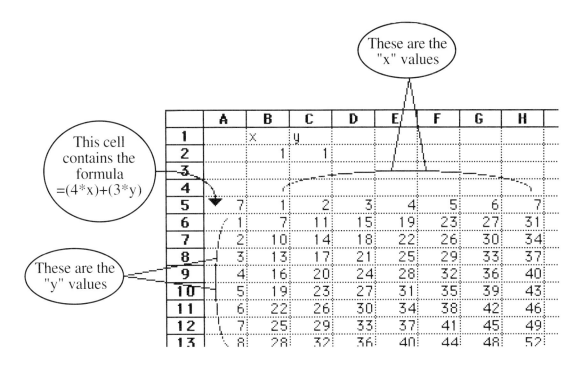

Fig. 5.9: Use of a table in EXCEL.

87

Chapter 6 CONCLUSIONS

As we come to finish this book we have been inundated with further ideas for using a spreadsheet package for mathematics: ideas involving calculus; ideas for teaching about the approximate nature of computer calculations; ideas for using with data handling. We were tempted to incorporate all these new ideas into the book until we remembered that we set out with the aim of providing problems to 'get started' in the classroom. These new ideas have all been generated by teachers who have used the materials in this book and this confirms our belief that the potential of a spreadsheet package for learning mathematics is still untapped.

We hope that spreadsheets will be used to help pupils develop and extend mathematical understandings in a way which will ultimately change the established expectation of pupils. In our opinion the new National Curriculum neither takes account of the effect which computer environments will have on pupils' mathematical understandings nor of the effect which computer environments are having on mathematics itself. This could enshrine both an outdated mathematics and an outdated expectation of pupils' mathematical development. At this stage all we can hope is that as teachers you will keep an open mind about the effects of a spreadsheet environment on both your teaching and your pupils' learning and that you do not destroy the potential of a spreadsheet environment by too rigorously trying to fit spreadsheets into the National Curriculum.

All the materials in this book have been tried out with pupils from a range of ages and we cannot stress enough how much our expectations of pupils have been challenged by observing pupils working in a spreadsheet environment. We have recently been using Find the Formula (Activity 2.1) with 10-year-olds and these pupils have surprised us with their confidence and facility with both the spreadsheet environment and the mathematical ideas involved. The possibility of generating sequences using both a recurrence and a universal rule is an idea which is normally confusing to pupils and which is dealt with in a fragmented way in the standard mathematics curriculum. When we tried out Two Ways of Expressing a Sequence (Activity 4.5) with lower secondary school pupils, we noticed that they were beginning to use the more natural recurrence rule (i.e. add 3 to the term before) to provide them with support in generating a universal rule. Finally the Activity Strange Behaviour and Chaos (Activity 4.8) can be used to make accessible ideas from the new branch of mathematics called Chaotic Dynamics.

A spreadsheet environment can be thought of as some sort of intermediary between natural and formal language. Pupils are able to enter a mathematical formula by physically moving the mouse or arrow keys without having to take on board all the complexities of a formal language. Nevertheless they have to be aware of the need for precision in their formalising, a crucial idea which has been underplayed during the last few decades of mathematics teaching. Many studies have found that pupils find algebraic symbolism difficult and alienating and so the use of symbolism in mathematics has become delayed and for some pupils almost completely removed. When faced with a problem in a spreadsheet environment pupils do not show the same reluctance and fear of symbolism which they exhibit in a 'normal' algebra environment and this is why we have chosen to focus most of the activities within this book around algebraic and related arithmetic ideas. We think that working in a spreadsheet environment will help pupils develop confidence and competence in algebra, inevitably affecting all their mathematics learning. It is our belief that most of the seemingly difficult algebraic ideas can be tackled within a spreadsheet environment, the most important of these being the idea of negotiating and expressing a generalisation within a formal language. Although our interests (Healy et al, 1990; Sutherland, 1990) are predominanly in the area of algebra, the spreadsheet also provides a rich environment for exploring arithmetical ideas and for helping to reinstate the important relationship between algebra and arithmetic. When the graphing facilities of spreadsheet packages improve, the spreadsheet environment can be used to help pupils make links between symbolic and graphical representations in algebra, allowing for the possibility of these two representations to be presented simultaneously.

It is never possible to anticipate the ways in which a new computer environment can be used to express and explore mathematical ideas, until this environment begins to be integrated into normal teaching practice. We are optimistic that pupils themselves will be able to lead the way. We end with a quote from two pupils discussing how a spreadsheet environment helped them express their mathematical ideas.

Sineád: *'It used to be awful...I used to try...trying to explain is really hard, but if you've got this it's much easier don't you think? I wish I had one of these at home so that I could do my investigations on it..it'd be a lot easier.'*

Natalie: *'Now you know how to think it out like a computer would.....so it should be easier....'*

Sineád: *'Oh well...next time you see I'll put all my numbers like this, 'cos it's a lot easier.....makes sense....'*

Bibliography

Catterall, P (1986) "More Mathematics with Multiplan", Micromath, Vol. 2, No. 2.

Devlin, K. (1988) Mathematics: The New Golden Age, Penguin Books.

Futcher, D. (1988) "Start with a Clean Sheet", New Educational Computing, June.

Gleick, J. (1988) Chaos, Heinemann.

Healy, L. & Sutherland, R. (1990) Using Spreadsheets within the Mathematics Classroom, International Journal of Mathematical Education in Science and Technology, Vol. 21, No. 6.

Hoyles, C. & Sutherland, R. (1989) Logo Mathematics in the Classroom, Routledge.

Hoyles, C., Sutherland, R & Healy, L (in press) Children Talking in Computer Environments: New Insights on the Role of Discussion in Mathematics Learning. In Durkin, K. & Shire, B.(eds) Language and Mathematical Education

NCET Publication Thinking about spreadsheets, NCET, University of Warwick, Science Park, Coventry.

Peasey, D. (1985) "Using Spreadsheet Programs in Mathematics Education", Micromath, Vol. 1., No. 1.

Peitgen, H.O., & Richter, P.H. (1986) The Beauty of Fractals, Springer-Verlag.

Rodick. A. (1984) "Some Surprising Iterations", The Mathematical Gazette, Vol. 68.

Scott, H. (1987) "Thinking Things Through", Micromath, Vol. 3, No. 2.

Stewart, I. (1989) Does God Play Dice, The Mathematics of Chaos, Penguin Books.

Sutherland, R. (1990) The Changing Role of Algebra in School Mathematics, In: Dowling, P. and Noss, R., Mathematics versus the National Curriculum, Kogan page.

Waddingham, J. & Wigley, A. (1985) Algebra and Algorithms, Secondary Mathematics with Micros In-service Pack.

Wright, S. (1987) "Classroom Uses for Spreadsheets", Micromath, Vol. 3., No. 2.